SUBTEXT

Julius Fast

SUBTEXT

MAKING BODY LANGUAGE WORK

IN THE WORKPLACE

VIKING

VIKING
Published by the Penguin Group
Viking Penguin, a division of Penguin Books USA Inc.,
375 Hudson Street, New York, New York 10014, U.S.A.
Penguin Books Ltd, 27 Wrights Lane,
London W8 5TZ, England
Penguin Books Australia Ltd, Ringwood, Victoria, Australia
Penguin Books Canada Ltd, 2801 John Street,
Markham, Ontario, Canada L3R 1B4
Penguin Books (N.Z.) Ltd, 182–190 Wairau Road,
Auckland 10, New Zealand

Penguin Books Ltd, Registered Offices:
Harmondsworth, Middlesex, England

First published in 1991 by Viking Penguin,
a division of Penguin Books USA Inc.

1 3 5 7 9 10 8 6 4 2

Grateful acknowledgment is made for permission to reprint "Prologue: The Birth of Architecture" from
"Thanksgiving for a Habitat" from *W. H. Auden: Collected Poems* by W. H. Auden. Copyright © 1963
by W. H. Auden. Reprinted by permission of Random House, Inc.

LIBRARY OF CONGRESS CATALOGING IN PUBLICATION DATA
Fast, Julius
Subtext : Making body language work in the workplace / Julius Fast.
p.   cm.
Includes index.
ISBN 0-670-83238-3
1. Communication in personnel management.   2. Interpersonal
communication.   I. Title.
HF5549.5.C6F37   1991
650.1′3—dc20   90-50466

Printed in the United States of America
Set in Bodoni Book
Designed by Beth Tondreau Design / Mary A. Wirth

FOR

BARBARA

ACKNOWLEDGMENTS

I would like to express my debt and gratitude to the many people who have helped me so generously with their time and knowledge. They are too many to list individually, but among them, I must thank the following:

Edward Lubell
Walter Pfister
Joyce Grillo
Anthony Thompson, OBE
Deborah Howard
Ingrid Ehrenberg
Edward Jaworowski

CONTENTS

CONTENTS

CONTENTS

SUBTEXT

SUBTEXT

In any exchange between two people or within a group, messages are communicated not only through what is said, but also through the underlying dynamics of what is *not* said: the subtext. Subtext is a kind of covert language that may add to the spoken text, reinforcing it and strengthening it; or may contradict the text, canceling out any promises or agreements.

A salesman, for example, might promise to deliver his product on a definite date, but his subtext lets his customer know "There's no way I can meet this deadline."

Maybe the boss promises her employees big bonuses if the business continues the way it's going, but her subtext may also be saying "I have no confidence at all that sales will continue at this rate."

And what about the junior executive who tells the CEO, "I'll have this report done tomorrow"? In spite of those confident words, the real message might be "Now I'm going to have to find a really clever excuse to stall another day!"

I was introduced to subtextual communication years ago when I was hired by a psychological research outfit to act as consultant on an experiment in counseling. In an attempt to get better results, the research team was videotaping interviews between counselors and disturbed children, then playing the tapes back so the counselors could see themselves in action.

I remember one session in which the counselor, a woman, sat across from a ten-year-old girl. The counselor's legs were crossed, and her body was pulled back, her posture tight and restricted. She seemed to be putting as much physical distance as she could between herself and the child.

The girl was abnormally shy, answering only in monosyllables, refusing to meet the counselor's eye—a disappointing interview, to say the least.

The counselor told us later, "I couldn't get anywhere with that one. She resisted me every inch of the way!"

When we talked to the girl alone, she said, "I don't like the lady who talked to me."

"Why not?"

"Because she didn't like me!"

My project director explained to the counselor and me, "Two subtexts are at work here. The child's subtext blatantly declared no cooperation. And yours"—she nodded at the counselor—"spelled out distaste and arrogance. What I'd like you to do now is sit down and watch the tape of the interview. Watch it carefully!"

We ran the tape of the interview for her, and the counselor was shocked. "I never realized how tight I was, how rejecting my whole posture was! No wonder she wouldn't look me in the eye!"

"At your next session," the director suggested, "why not loosen up. lean forward, touch the little girl's hand, and let's see what happens."

A second session was held, and the counselor followed the director's advice, making an effort to lean forward, and to keep her posture more relaxed. The child responded by looking up and making eye contact. But the real turning point was when the counselor put her hand on top of the child's. It was as if something in the child melted, and what poured out was exactly what the counselor had hoped for.

"I thought the counselor's loosening up would change the interview," I told the director, "but I had no idea it would change it so drastically!"

She nodded. "When two or more people interact, there's always the obvious text and the more subtle—and incidentally, more honest—subtext."

The subtext in any exchange is a mixture of many different elements. In part, it is composed of each person's body language, posture, hand movements, eye contact, how he or she handles space, and the ability to use subtle touch at the right moment. The way we use our voices also influences how our words are interpreted. The same sentence can be said in many different ways, ranging from bland disinterest to passionate intensity. Each delivery spells out a different subtext.

For instance, when former president Jimmy Carter spoke off the cuff his normal speech pattern lent a pleasant, down-home, and honest subtext to his words. When he spoke formally, however, before an audience or for television, his voice became stilted and he would pause at awkward intervals, sending a message of uncertainty and uneasiness.

Who knows? Proper coaching might have changed his speaking pattern and subtext, perhaps increasing his popularity, and eventually changing the course of history.

In contrast, the subtext behind former president Ronald Reagan's speech pattern was one of ease and reassurance. It sent the message "I'm a good fellow. You can trust and like me." Maybe his acting career had shown him the value of subtext in communication and how it can affect an audience.

The image we project is another form of subtext. How many of us have walked down a city street and watched uneasily as a group of young men in ripped jeans and leather jackets have come toward us? Are they ordinary, harmless citizens, we wonder, or is there something threatening about them? Is there reason to be apprehensive, or should we shrug our feelings off? The same group approaching us in business suits and ties would arouse no such apprehension. Why? Quite simply, they would project a different subtext, one that's reassuring and ordinary.

In most established businesses, such as law firms and brokerage houses, there is a rigid protocol of dress. Your appearance, the thinking goes, should inspire confidence in your customers; the subtext should be one of assurance, one that will convince clients that you are a solid professional, and that they are in competent hands.

However, in some industries, the clothes you wear may be selected to say something completely different. I have a neighbor who runs an advertising agency; all his clients are in the music business. He's very successful—a limo picks him up and takes him to work each day—but I have never seen him wear anything but well-washed jeans, a shirt with no tie, and a casual sport jacket. His subtext? "You can trust me because I'm not uptight!"

Even the way we eat influences the message we send, as many corporations are discovering. As one CEO told me, "I have this incredibly bright, well-educated guy who really has a grasp of the business. Well, we had lunch with an important client and he ate like an animal, shoveling food into his mouth without the slightest regard for appearance!"

"What do you mean by appearance?" I asked.

"Why, the message he was sending to the client! In effect, he was saying, I don't know the rules for eating properly. How can I know the rules for interacting with people?" He shook his head. "You may not believe it, but now we have sessions with our upcoming executives to teach them the proper way to behave at the table!"

Again, it's a matter of subtext. Not knowing how to handle oneself properly in the executive dining room or at a business lunch can contradict the image of competence a professional person wants to project.

Subtextual messages also differ according to gender. For example, women are usually better at expressing warmth through their facial expressions. In business their smiles and nods can communicate friendliness and openness; their graceful ease with their own bodies sends a ready subtext of sincerity. Men have different advantages. They are more comfortable with handshakes, and the casual touch, and it's easier for them to make eye contact. These are all social skills related to the roles men are taught to play in society.

Another kind of subtext is related to regional or national speech patterns. We tend to trust the sound of our own regional accent and listen with suspicion to that of another. A New Yorker in Middle America may carry the baggage of a distinctive accent. He or she is immediately suspect. Conversely, the Midwesterner or New Englander in New York City might send out a subtext of naïveté, no matter how smart he or she is. The point is, we are uneasy with subtexts that differ from our own, and we tend to treat the "other" with suspicion, contempt, or, in some cases, unwarranted respect.

Most people subconsciously perceive and understand subtexts in others. They meet someone who, on the surface, seems friendly and cooperative, but underneath they sense an entirely different personality. For some reason, they don't trust the person, although the mistrust is not based on anything concrete. What they have done is sense a contradictory subtext.

That feeling can be brought up to the conscious level. With the help of this book, you will no longer have to say "There's something about her that I don't trust, but don't ask me what," or "I'm not sure why I like him despite his touchiness." You will learn to understand the underlying message and bring it to the fore.

Knowing and understanding the elements of subtext will also allow you to change your own to match what you really want to project. Take the case of Lisa, who was hired as an assistant by one of the stockbrokers in a large Chicago firm. She was promised that eventually she would work her way up in the company. "There are tremendous opportunities for someone with your skills and competence," her boss assured her, but a year in the same rut, with no sign of promotion or salary increase, began to demoralize her.

"Your problem," her superior told her frankly, "is the way you interact with your clients. You know your stuff, but . . ." He shrugged. "Somehow you don't project confidence, and your sales record shows it."

Thoroughly crushed, Lisa turned to her friend Karen for advice. Karen was hired at the same time, but was far ahead of Lisa on the corporate ladder. "I've been watching you," Karen said, "and I believe it's your general attitude. You sit with a customer, slumped forward, your head down—why, you hardly ever make eye contact. Are you afraid of the customers?"

Lisa sighed. "I guess I am. I'm going to have to face the fact that much as I want the job, I'm in the wrong field. When I talk to the clients I feel uneasy, anxious that I'm giving the wrong advice. So much is riding on the investments I suggest!"

"That's a crock!" Karen told her. "Your advice is a hundred percent great. Look, let's do a little body language reconstruction. Try sitting up straight, leaning forward, making eye contact and, yes, even smiling!"

Lisa watched Karen at work and began imitating her posture, her movements. To her surprise, she found that sitting and moving in an affirmative way increased, to a small extent, her confidence in herself and the advice she was giving. It became easier to take a more affirmative posture, and in turn her positive feelings grew greater. She entered a kind of circular feedback where, as the confidence she projected through subtext grew, her inward feelings of confidence increased as well. One fed on the other, and by the year's end she had been promoted to the next level.

Dr. Robert Zajonic, a psychologist at the University of Michigan, has uncovered evidence of a physiological basis to what Lisa discovered—that convincingly changing the subtext you project can affect your mood and attitude. As facial muscles relax or tighten, the temperature of blood flowing to the brain is raised or lowered. These changes in temperature in turn affect the brain centers that regulate emotions.

As proof, Dr. Zajonic had volunteers repeat certain vowel sounds over and over. A long "e," which forces a smile, and "ah," which imitates the expression of surprise, both induced pleasant feelings. Other sounds, such as a long "u," put volunteers into a bad mood.

A team of psychologists at Clark University in Worcester, Massachussets, found confirming evidence for Dr. Zajonic's theory. Like Dr. Zajonic, they showed that facial expressions indicating disgust, anger, fear, or surprise indeed aroused those emotions. The expression caused the mood! Simply stated, looking happy makes you feel happy. Looking sad makes you feel sad.

Dr. Paul Ekman and other psychologists at the University of California Medical School in San Francisco went a step further. They showed that when people mimic different emotions, they actually experience distinct physiological reactions, such as changes in body temperature and breathing rates.

In these and other instances, science is catching up with folk wisdom, which tells us to "put on a happy face" or "walk tall." The very act of changing your expression or your posture starts a chain reaction that makes you actually experience change, which makes it even easier to "look the part."

Changing your subtext by changing your behavior gives strength and validity to your text.

1

WHAT YOU SEE
IS NOT WHAT
YOU GET

MAKING AN IMPRESSION

Sometimes, it's not what's on the inside, but what is on the outside that counts in projecting a subtext. External techniques can be just as important as inner personality traits in producing an image, especially when it comes to interviewing for a job, making a sale, or closing a deal.

A winner of the prestigious Westinghouse Science Award came

up with a very clever project which illustrates the point. Mina Chow, a young Korean-American girl who attended Cardozo High School in New York City, noticed that teachers base a lot of grades on a student's image, on what students look like. Mina originally looked like a typical "punk" kid with spiked hair and blue lipstick. Her grades were slipping until she decided on an image change. She toned herself down to a more average appearance, and her grades went up. "I figured that the teachers' perceptions had a lot to do with it," Mina realized.

Mina elaborated on her own perceptions for a science project. She collected "neutral" pictures of black, white, and Asian students, male and female, and distributed them along with a questionnaire to eighty-seven teachers in New York City high schools.

The results scored a big point for the subtext behind image projection. Asian students were rated highest for motivation, blacks the lowest. Blacks were rated highest for physical activity, Asians the lowest. Mina concluded that Asians might do better in school simply because teachers had preconceived notions about them.

We all carry preconceived notions around with us. Certainly, in an ideal world, we would judge people by what they do, not by their race or clothes or social status, but this is not an ideal world, and we judge others by the images they project.

Nowhere is this more true than in television. In 1987, during the Senate confirmation hearings of Judge Robert H. Bork for the U.S. Supreme Court, John Dancy, a TV correspondent, said of the Bork hearings, "The wind blows from the image." According to John Corry, the *New York Times* television critic, Judge Bork "looks like a Reform rabbi, and speaks like an Oxford don." He went on to note that Bork's constitutional interpretation is "as interesting as origami folding. How one looks, however, is something else. Appearance is what counts."

In business, as well as in television, how one looks becomes all important. There are lessons that businesspeople can learn from television techniques.

CREATING THE RIGHT IMAGE
FOR ANY SITUATION

A statement by Michael K. Deaver, who used to manage President Reagan's news conferences, holds a key to projecting an image with a serious and dramatic subtext. Deaver had Reagan stand in front of the open doors of the East Room for press conferences, because it made the president appear livelier and more substantive. "The open doors with the light coming across the hall makes a much better picture," Mr. Deaver told reporters. Moving the lectern away from the open door was, in Mr. Deaver's opinion, unwise—telegenically speaking.

In politics, we see an example of subtext at work. How the president looks sends a strong subtext to the television viewer no matter what he says! Margaret Mead, the great anthropologist, was aware of this. She once told me that her advice to President Carter was, "It doesn't matter what you say. What's important is how you look."

Television critic John Corry recognized the importance of subtext in politics. He pointed out that Reagan's campaign used visual effects that were very strong and sent a clear image of patriotism. There were flags, waving placards, balloons rising up in clouds, and, at his 1981 inaugural, the Mormon Tabernacle Choir singing "The Battle Hymn of the Republic." President Reagan himself was so moved that he cried. It worked!

The paradox of television campaigning, according to John Corry, is that what is real always works better than artifice. The president's tears worked. However, combine reality with carefully planned presentation, and you have a compelling subtext!

Unfortunately, television can create an artificial subtext that is often accepted as real. Viewers can be moved, not by the issue, but by the projected image. The candidate may be an empty shell, but that doesn't matter. Is the candidate too cold, too remote? Let that person appear before the camera as one of us, as a common man or woman. Is there some doubt about the candidate's patriotism? Let that candidate appear before the memorial of the flag raising at Iwo Jima, or even in a flag factory. The strong subtext will carry him or her through.

In the business world, the same rules apply. Is the boss seen as too cold, too far removed? Let him or her appear at a plant inspection in work clothes and a hard hat—a warm, caring subtext!

We must never underestimate the strength of image projection, nor how much seemingly obvious and calculated mechanisms can move people. Politics, with its finely tuned communication directors, takes the lead. In the eighties we had Reagan's "Morning in America" commercials; their warm, fuzzy, golden, glowing, and sentimental patriotic images sent out a solid subtext of "I love America."

Representative Jack F. Kemp jumped on the same patriotic bandwagon. He used a commercial that opened with "Hometown, USA." Golden sunlight illuminates the streets at dawn. A newsboy tosses a paper at a porch. A woman opens her shop. A fireman hoses down his truck—and, in case the message still eludes some dim viewers, someone runs up the American flag.

And, of course, the subtext hits home: patriotism, American values, family values. These are all linked, by subtext, to the candidate.

Politicians learn from business because they hire the same public-relations firms that business uses. Mr. Kemp hired BBDO International of New York, the same firm that created the Reagan commercials.

What we see in these commercials is an unusual distancing. The candidate no longer needs to project his or her own subtext. Instead, a series of video pictures projects it. The pictures make us smile, nod in agreement, and end up with a catch in our throat. Put the candidate's name after the pictures, and even his or her image is not necessary. It is subtext once removed.

How many commercial ads have we seen that employ the same technique? How about ads for cereals that show a hazy early morning in Anytown, USA, a kitchen bathed in golden sunlight, smiling, happy people—a warm, kind America eating breakfast cereal. Or on a stronger note, consider ads depicting beautiful women, handsome men, and sleek new cars. Women and cars, men and cars, cars tearing along at speeds we can never reach on the highway: What are they telling us? Advertisers hope viewers will respond to the subtext of power and sexuality rather than to any facts about the car itself. Recently, a subtle television ad for a new car used only subtext with not even a picture of the car. Images of breaking waves, lightning bolts, and other natural phenomena denoted power and harmony, then the name of the car was whispered with awe. The subtext does it all!

Turning to politics again for another lesson, consider the way President Reagan used the setting of the White House. In 1986, a newspaper reporter wrote that Reagan would emerge from behind a closed door, stride purposefully down a long, red-carpeted corridor, then fairly bound onto a platform. The subtext was communicated before he spoke: vigor, authority, and ease.

A clever executive can walk into a conference room with that same attitude. Those who can do it send out a subtext of *I'm in charge here.* The confident walk, the physical energy, and the relaxed style all work together.

PUT ON THE MASK

Marshall McLuhan once said, "TV will not take a face. It has to have a mask." *Face,* in this statement, is "the expression that projects the personality." *Mask* means an expression that reveals very little about the person.

TV talk-show host Morton Downey, Jr., appeared without a mask, in all the rawness of his personality. The audience saw the abrasive character of the man and soon grew tired of him. They felt they knew all they needed to know. There was no subtext to uncover; what you saw was what you got.

On the other hand, people like Johnny Carson assume a mask; in Carson's case, a faintly bemused expression. Viewers are never sure that they know the real Carson, and so he is always intriguing.

Ted Koppel, who hosts ABC's "Nightline" program, also wears a television mask, a rather bland one. "Such a mask," Mr. Koppel has said, pleases the viewer who "watches me and . . . chooses to believe that I believe what he believes."

How do you develop such a mask for television or business? According to Mr. Koppel, it's a question of toning down your own views, of not getting trapped in an inflexible image, and of not allowing others to think that they've got you figured out.

It is not easy to assume an unreadable mask. Take Vice President Dan Quayle, for example. In an article in the Sunday *New York Times,* writer Philip Marchand suggested that for Quayle to escape from his subtextual image as an inexperienced lightweight—a subtext that friends see as guilelessness and enemies perceive as dim-wittedness—the vice president should take a lesson from Mr. Koppel. That lesson could be summed up in three points: (1) Don't smile; (2) look as if you've seen and heard it all before; (3) don't make speeches.

These are interesting points, particularly since most people who give advice about subtexts advocate smiling. The smile is the most direct way of saying "I like you," "I'm happy in your presence." It conveys a subtext of trust and caring. In the case of someone like the vice president, however, it has an unhappy effect. It seems a bit juvenile for his station, too simple. A serious mask would convey a better subtext.

The second point made by Mr. Marchand, "look as if you've seen and heard it all before," signals a subtext of competence, of being in charge. Along with an unsmiling face, this subtext is easily conveyed by a raised eyebrow and a shrug.

In Dan Quayle's case, the advice not to make formal speeches is particularly applicable. While his off-the-cuff speaking style is acceptable, his formal prepared speeches tend to slip into a high school debating style, according to Mr. Marchand. The authoritative voice is lost.

Mr. Marchand advises politicians to let people "see themselves in the mask they wear." The advice we give to politicians seeking to send effective subtextual messages applies just as well to executives and CEOs.

In Vice President Quayle's case, it means suppressing that "boyish" smile. In the case of an older man, a man who has achieved a serious and sincere image, it means allowing the smile to become part of the mask. On the executive level, it is important not to be trapped in a predictable image. Do not allow others to believe they've "got you figured." A certain subtext of mystery will create uncertainty in your opponent. The mystery is created by the mask, the mask that signals "I'm unguessable."

THE JANUS FACTOR

Civilization, to a large degree, is based on masking, or its first cousin, control. When people live together and work together, a great deal of their day is spent covering up what they really feel and in controlling their real emotions. It may seem surprising, but sometimes it is very important to mask the subtexts we send out, to keep what we really feel hidden.

Sometimes the masking is consistent, but more often than not it is based on what I call the Janus Factor. Janus, you will remember, was the Roman god represented with two opposite faces. Jake is a perfect example of the Janus Factor in action.

Jake's job is to supervise a dozen workers in his department. "One thing about Jake," one of the people under him said, "he's consistent. A grade-A bully every time!"

The executives above Jake couldn't believe the occasional negative reports they heard about him. "This is a very sweet guy," his immediate superior insisted. "He's always ready to do a favor, always helpful and pleasant. Gets his job done quickly. There must be a couple of bad apples in that crew of his."

Was Jake two different people? A dual personality? Not at all. He simply used the Janus Factor to cope with life. In essence, the Janus Factor says that every man or woman in a corporation has two faces. One face is turned toward the people higher up in the corporate structure, and sends out one type of subtext. Another face is turned toward those lower down, with quite a different subtext.

A corollary of the Janus Factor is that the more secure the person is in the corporate structure, the less difference there is between the two faces and the two subtexts. The president of Jake's company seems to have only one face, but of course no one at work sees the face he presents to his wife and children.

The Janus factor is best observed in industry, but it also applies to politics. In the Watergate affair, the nation saw one face of President Nixon and received one subtext—a calm, rational man in control. The secret tapes disclosed a completely different face—vulgar and out of control. Were the two faces one man? Certainly. It was the Janus Factor in action.

Of course, just about every president has two faces. President Bush, when he was vice president, wore a subservient face. Now, as top dog, he makes it plain that no one is telling him what to do.

WEARING THE MASK

What is important about the Janus Factor in business, in politics, and even in the family is learning when and how to mask, to cover up your real emotions and the subtexts they send out. Politicians must learn this lesson early on. Edmund Muskie was destroyed as a possible presidential candidate by crying in public, letting the mask drop. On the other hand, when television evangelist Tammy Faye Bakker cried openly, she was using tears as a mask.

Doctors must learn to mask in front of patients; lawyers must wear a mask in court. The higher you climb on the corporate ladder, the more important the mask becomes. The simplest mask is the noncommittal look, the expressionless face. But expression itself is a much better masking device.

Lack of expression sends a negative subtext—"No one is home." An expression of any kind sends a positive subtext: joy, anger, fear, hate, whatever. A smile is the easiest way to mask unhappiness, anger, or disappointment. It sends a pleasant subtext. A grim look can mask joy and elation; a frown can cover up happiness.

Some of us use more than expressions to mask. Women use makeup to emphasize their lips and eyes, create a blush on their cheeks. Men use hair to mask: a full moustache can be a virility mask; a beard can change the contour of the face, strengthen a receding chin, add a subtext of wisdom, of cool.

When does masking start? As far as we know, it is present in early childhood. Most children approach strange adults with solemn faces and wary eyes, giving little of themselves, holding back their true feelings. The bright child learns quickly what adults expect and masks accordingly.

When children discover that their own feelings are not acceptable to society, they have the choice of changing those feelings or covering them up—masking. In most cases feelings can't be changed, so the child covers them up and creates a secret, inner world of emotions and fantasies.

Teenagers become even more adept at masking as their changing bodies release a flood of hormones that sharpens their desires and needs. They don't dare reveal those needs, and yet they are not nearly as adept at masking as grown-ups. As a compromise, they usually dredge up the noncommittal mask of childhood, or hide behind a sullen look. Unfortunately, the subtexts sent out are not *I'm upset, I'm in trouble!* but *I don't give a damn!*

Parents and teachers write off teenage sullenness as typical of the child at that age, but behind the sullen mask there may be a sensitive person—too tender, frightened, and vulnerable to face the world. The mask and its subtext are a way of protecting that fragile interior.

USING THE MASK

If we consider all the situations in which we use the masking technique, we can realize what a universal device it is to send out subtext, or rather, not send a subtext. Politeness, something we think of as a civilized pleasure of our culture, is simply an elaborate form of masking. We use masking constantly in business, at school, at home, with our enemies, and with our friends. When it comes right down to it, very few of us will dare to expose our inner selves by sending out the subtext of our true feelings.

This inner self is the most sacred part of us, and we are not expected to reveal it. Masking these feelings is important, provided the masking is kept within reasonable limits. In fact, showing our true feelings can be wrong and selfish.

Sandy, in charge of training in the computer department of her firm, explained this in terms of her relationship to her trainees. "I can't tell them the truth about their work in the beginning. It would be counterproductive. Sure, they make some stupid mistakes and I point out the obvious ones, but I can't let them see how exasperated I get. I must encourage them, and as long as they understand the subtext of encouragement behind what I say, they'll keep on trying. If they think they're doing well, they'll go on to do better."

Sandy's training technique was a form of masking. Sid, a foreman on the production line, used a similar technique. "I never tell the new guys how klutzy they are. I tell them they're doing fine, build them up, and they lose their nervousness and actually do better. I guess I put on an act, but it encourages them to keep at it. I turn out some good people that way."

CONTROL

Another aspect of masking is control, something we need in order to adapt to life in a civilized society. We need to control our basic desires to take what we want, to do what we want, even to live and work as we want. The modification of want is what control is all about.

We learn control at an early age. Hungry babies scream until the bottle comes, but gradually they learn to control their hunger, to wait for food at appropriate times. They learn to control their bladder and bowels as they grow up, then learn to control their desires and suppress those that are antisocial.

The act of learning control can be pleasant, because along with control the growing child learns anticipation with all its joys. The gradual refinement of control and the suppression of drives and desires are steps to maturity. We even define the subtext of immaturity as a lack of control.

Immature children who can't or won't learn control are hard to live with. When they want something, they want it at once. When they feel angry, they cry or yell or throw a tantrum. When they're hungry, they beg for food. If they're old enough to get their own food, they eat erratically with no regard for regular hours.

Gavin was that kind of a child, and not much better as an adult. He was unlucky enough to have parents who gave in easily and catered to his lack of control. When he moved out on his own, his apartment became as messy as his room at home, junk and clothes everywhere.

For a brief period he shared his apartment, and his life, with a young woman, but it didn't last. "I can't live like that. I'm not that neat, but to just drop everything everywhere and wonder where it is when you want it! And meals. I plan dinner at seven and at six you're hungry so you fill up on junk food!"

Gavin shrugged. "Why not eat when you're hungry? I'm hungry at six. Why wait till seven?"

"Because I go to a lot of trouble to prepare dinner at seven! Can't you control your hunger?"

Obviously Gavin couldn't, and finally his girlfriend moved out. He was upset, but not enough to change. "Why do I have to be uptight about everything? It's not my life-style!"

But his life-style spilled over into his work. He started a good job with an outfit making documentaries for cable television, but he could no more control his work than he could control his life. He misplaced important documents, neglected dull projects, failed to change scripts, and eventually lost his job.

It's difficult, he discovered, to be controlled on one level while you're out of control on another. To be effective, control must be exhibited in most areas of your life.

Sometimes we find a deceptive charm about uncontrolled people. The subtext they send out is romantic, above commonplace demands, even primitive and natural, but they are difficult to live with and next to impossible to work with—or, worse still, to work for!

Few people are controlled in every area, but most people use degrees of control to send out a subtext of sensibility and order. The ones who can't or won't are the gamblers who never resist a long shot: the person who buys the too-expensive car because "even if I don't need it, it looks great"; the thief who can't resist an easy setup; or the dieter who must have that extra piece of cake.

SOME ADVICE FROM A PRO

Walter J. Pfister, Jr., is president of the Executive Television Workshop. A former vice president of news for ABC, Mr. Pfister is a veteran of twenty-five years in network television. He produced six national political conventions and covered five national elections. Currently, he trains leading executives and spokespeople in presenting the correct subtext in TV interviews, speeches, presentations, and board meetings.

During a recent conversation with Mr. Pfister, he told me, "Television has changed the world in terms of image projection and subtext in any business encounter. The first impression you form of somebody is the most important one. Ten minutes after a presentation, no matter how inspiring, ask someone who heard it to jot down what was said, and he may be able to come up with one or two topic sentences. That's about it. But ask, were you at ease with the speaker? Did you like him? Did you believe him? Did you think he was sincere? Would you trust him? Ask those questions and they'll have definite impressions. They'll answer with much more certainty!"

It's the image that counts, according to Mr. Pfister, because the image transmits the subtext. "Take political debates. If you look at the text of any of them you'll find that they're pretty meager. No one says anything of substance. What matters is the impression on the audience and their reaction to the speaker's subtext. Did

I like this candidate or didn't I? It's sad, but unfortunately it's true."

I asked Mr. Pfister how, in a business situation, one can make the right impression. How, for example, do you send out a subtext of confidence?

Smile, was his first suggestion. "Someone gets up to address a board meeting, and often he or she is too flat, too nervous, or just frightened. The board senses that, just the way animals sense fear. The same is true for one-on-one meetings."

Remembering Philip Marchand's advice to Dan Quayle, I asked Mr. Pfister how he reconciled this with his own advice about smiling.

"That's a special case. Of course the wrong sort of smile, the too eager and boyish one, may send out a subtext of callow youth. In that case, you either change your smile or ease up on it.

"In any business situation," he stressed, "it's very important to look as comfortable as you can. A smile certainly helps. Another way of transmitting comfort and ease is to use the other person's first name. The first name, far from offending, puts the other person at ease, and creates a subtext of friendliness. To keep that subtext going, be conversational. Don't speechify or lecture, even if you're addressing a group. Remember, the shorter your talk, the better. It's not so much what you say as the way that you say it!"

I wondered if it didn't take a lot of practice for executives to learn these rules, but Mr. Pfister shook his head. "You'd be amazed at how quickly executives in large companies learn. Executives must be leaders. The better they are at communicating, the more they know about transmitting the exact subtext they're after, and the better they are at leading. The executive in the ivory tower is a thing of the past."

What about executives interacting with people above or below them in the corporate hierarchy? Should they vary their style?

"You should talk neither down nor up to someone. You have to be yourself," he said firmly. "Ask permission to use your boss's first name. In most cases, he or she will agree."

On the other hand, don't walk in on someone you don't know and use his or her first name. The subtext, then, is one of crassness or arrogance. You must first get an indication of how that person feels about being on such a friendly basis with you.

Dealing with a subordinate is an even more tenuous situation. "If you're talking to the foreman of the shop and you wish to give him a sense of dignity," Pfister says, "address him as mister. The subtext is respect."

DO CLOTHES MAKE THE IMAGE?

As for the subtext of dressing, clothes do make a big difference in how you are perceived. In Walter Pfister's opinion, neatness, cleanliness, and appropriateness are the all-important factors. While he believes certain colors in men's clothes are "power colors," he also feels that most business advisers have gone overboard on the subject. "Say the shop foreman comes in to see the chairman of the board. For him to get dressed up in a blue suit he only wears on Sunday is just not appropriate. But he certainly shouldn't come in with grease on his hands!"

I agree. There are colors that send a strong subtext, though it's nonsensical to think you can guarantee success by wearing them. What colors can do is help change your image. For men in the business world, dark blue, black, and charcoal gray are colors that project a subtext of strength and competence. White shirts and muted ties complete the image.

While women have a wider choice in clothes, men are usually advised to play it safe. Clifford Grodd, president of Paul Stuart, says that in business men should try to project a subtext of intelligence. They shouldn't appear overly involved with clothes unless they work in the fashion world.

In architecture, industrial design, publishing, or advertising, a sport jacket and slacks are generally acceptable. I have seen a number of young male executives in these creative fields wearing neat denim jeans with shirt, tie, and jacket.

The classic blue blazer with dark gray slacks, a white or even light blue shirt, and a dark, striped tie is an acceptable outfit in many business situations. "The dark trousers send a business subtext," Grodd says. "As long as you don't look as if you're going to a party at the yacht club!"

And Joyce Grillo, president of Impression Management image consultants, who has a background in psychology, has some strong ideas about women's clothes in the corporate world. She believes that the entire idea of dressing for success has been taken to extremes, especially for women.

"For men it's still the dark colors in suits, the white shirt, and the muted tie. Unfortunately, men are limited; brown, green, yellow, plaids—they are all out. Tan is not a decisive color, and light gray—well, some men can wear it depending on their coloring.

"For women, what they wear does, to an extent, depend on where they work, but today it's really wide open. In a sober industry, such as banking, brokerage, or law, women still need to dress in conservative colors. However, they can wear dresses instead of the suits that are generally advised, as long as it's the right kind of dress, a coat dress perhaps or something that looks like a jacket—nothing too frilly or cutesy. A dress can give the subtext of competence, which is the subtext a woman wants."

Ms. Grillo pointed out that there is no easy formula. "You can't go to a book on how to dress for success and follow a rigid pattern. It won't work. For one thing, those books are too conservative for today's world! For another, each woman must develop her personal style, a style that suits her own personality and subtext." She stresses that women in business should, above all, dress with quality. As for color, that depends on the situation. "If I were going into a bank in a business situation for the first time I would wear red. It's a very warm color and it stimulates people. It sends a subtext of confidence, and today it's as acceptable as navy for women. People like to look at it, and women like to wear it."

She listed yellow as another attractive but unappreciated color, warning, however, that women must find the shade of yellow that suits their particular complexions. "It's not an easy color, but it can be effective. I think green is another wonderful color, particularly teal."

The point she emphasized is that women in business can be a lot more creative today in terms of dress. They should develop their own style and be comfortable with what they wear. There are a lot of options available, but the businesswoman must be careful to avoid clothes that are too trendy or outlandish. The most important element in dressing for business is that the type of business will dictate the style of dress—and, in turn, your style of dress will dictate your subtext.

As an example, Ms. Grillo cited the area of sales where a subtext of credibility is the most important thing. "If you don't impress me as being credible, why should I buy from you? Why will I believe you're selling me something that works?"

The subtext of credibility comes not only from how you speak in the sales pitch itself, but also from how you dress. A saleswoman in an expensive urban department store such as Saks Fifth Avenue or Bergdorf Goodman would dress with high style and some degree of flash. In a store like Tiffany, which sells very expensive but traditional items, she would dress more conservatively—a tailored dress. In a store like L.L. Bean in Maine, where the outdoors is featured, jeans and a flannel shirt project credibility. A saleswoman selling real estate in Beverly Hills, where the prices run to the millions, might wear mink and diamonds, while a woman selling in a Rodeo Drive boutique could wear trendy high fashion.

Mara Urshel, senior vice president and senior merchandising manager of women's wear at Saks Fifth Avenue in New York City, believes that the most important rule of dressing for business is conformity. Know what everybody else is wearing "because that's what you're going to live with if you want to succeed." She agrees with Ms. Grillo that, in general, women have more options. The traditional matched suit is on its way out.

Louise Maniscalco, a personal shopper at Barneys in New York City, says, "Businesswomen can wear a jacket that goes with the skirt in terms of color, but that isn't necessarily the same design, color, or fabric or even made by the same designer."

She also suggests that women can wear offbeat outfits, depending on where they work. Women in conservative fields must still wear skirts and dresses. "Trousers and pants suits work in fashion, publishing, advertising, medicine, or real estate." She suggested that hemlines are up for grabs. They can be at the knee, mid-calf, or even longer, and with the new styles, they can even go above the knee.

An unmatched outfit—say, a mustard jacket, white blouse, and black skirt—is a versatile first purchase for a young business-woman. Unmatched suits are accepted, and a variety of jackets are useful to combine with different blouses and skirts for different effects. If the job is not too conservative and a jacket is not required, a vest gives an outfit polish and fashion savvy.

Working at home presents women with different subtext challenges. Most may dress more casually, but some still take time to apply makeup every morning.

Luci R. Knight, who operates a marketing office from her Pleasantville, New York, home, believes that wearing makeup gives her confidence and a business persona when she talks on the phone. "It makes a definite difference in how I come across," she claims.

Joyce Matz, a public-relations consultant in Manhattan who works out of her home, uses some makeup because "I like to have it on if the doorman or UPS man comes up." Some women find that wearing makeup helps them send out a subtext of professionalism.

Joyce Grillo sums it up: "When you dress up, even to work at home, you are more productive. Wear something that makes you feel good about yourself. The way you dress sends out a subtext of how you feel about yourself and your work."

HAIR—THE LONG AND SHORT OF IT

I asked Joyce Grillo about women's hair, and she suggested that in most business situations short, neat, and polished sends a subtext of competence. Long hair, while it is attractive, is often perceived as inappropriate in a business setting. As Ms. Grillo remarks on the paradox of hair in the workplace, "A lot of women tell me that when they cut their hair they feel freer, more aggressive, more energetic. Of course there are some who feel naked and vulnerable!"

There is, indeed, a strong subtext to hair. Most women have been brought up with long-haired fashion models and screen stars as their role models. Long hair is particularly fascinating to men, and women are made aware of this at an early age. Some women equate cutting their hair with losing their femininity, but worry that the image projected by long hair can be problematic in business. Of course, in some fields long hair is an asset. The cosmetic industry and the world of high fashion welcome the glamorous subtext sent by long hair, but also accept the particular chic of short hair. Increasingly, fashion models sport short cuts, especially when the subtext desired is slick, contemporary style.

In men, longer hair is becoming more acceptable in the workplace, but only on younger men. With older men, the hair is best cut short and neat. Long hair seems out of place. In balding men, combing the few remaining strands of hair to disguise the loss of hair is also unsuitable. The subtext implied is that of a man rather pathetically holding on to youth. In business, as in any realm of life, men and women should learn to age gracefully and accept the subtexts that an older appearance brings: among them, greater experience, expertise, and wisdom. If their dress and appearance are in keeping with their age, the subtexts will also be acceptable.

Accepting your age gracefully might mean avoiding pointless attempts at youth, but it certainly does not mean that you shouldn't take sensible steps to overcome certain biases against age. There is nothing wrong with avoiding gray hair by using hair coloring, provided it is done subtly; and plastic surgery has helped many men and women stay on in their jobs.

While changing your image to change your subtext works when your business has a bias against age, it also works when age is not a factor. Joyce Grillo tells of a man referred to her by a rather conservative corporation. He was very good at his job, which was in a technical field, and he was in his mid-forties. "Unfortunately, he knew nothing about clothes and cared even less. When I met him, he had a rumpled appearance. He needed a haircut and he was wearing slacks with a tear in them, a worn plaid sport jacket, a patterned shirt, and a flowered tie!"

Obviously he was aware that something was wrong with how he looked. He told Ms. Grillo that during his years at the company people had subtly mentioned his appearance. "I know I'm no fancy dresser, and I guess that's why the company hired you to talk to me, but I just don't want to spend much on my clothes. It's not worth it. I've got some money put aside, but my wife wants new kitchen cabinets and that's where the money's going to go!"

After some discussion, he settled on a budget that he was willing to spend on clothes. He and Ms. Grillo went shopping together and picked out a charcoal gray suit, white shirt, dark maroon tie, and new black shoes—and then to a barber for a conservative haircut. "Dressed in his new clothes," Ms. Grillo said with a smile, "he looked good—a very attractive man, though you wouldn't have guessed it before. The rumpled look was gone, along with its old subtext."

A week later he called Ms. Grillo. "You know," he told her, "I have to tell you something. I went to a meeting with some new people and they treated me differently from the way I've always been treated. They listened to me and I felt good about it. The same thing has been happening at the plant. People are relating to me better. It's a whole new experience!

"About the money for the kitchen cabinets, my wife and I agreed to put them on hold. Nobody's going to see my cabinets. I'm using the money to buy new clothes."

SUBTEXT AND THE LAW

In 1972, Bill Clark, a police officer in the Seventy-eighth Precinct in Brooklyn, was promoted to detective. His new colleagues suggested that he dress to fit his new role, so Bill went out and bought two double-knit suits, one raspberry and white, the other a flashy plaid, some striped shirts, and vivid ties.

The other detectives were startled, but finally one of them took him to a clothing wholesaler where a salesman helped him pick out a three-piece flannel suit. Despite television images of sloppily dressed New York City detectives, Bill Clark told a *New York* magazine reporter in 1984, police dress in New York is based on common sense. Detectives, he explained, try to project a subtext of dignity and even charm. Sometimes, dress can be even more important than their guns.

Things have changed since 1984 when Detective Clark was interviewed. Today the savvy city detective tries to project a tough street subtext. It's the best way of handling a drug-ridden city. However, in any precinct house you will still find detectives in business suits, in keeping with the more formal subtext.

Some time ago I was fortunate enough to be able to interview a group of Philadelphia trial lawyers. I showed up in my best outfit: a tweed jacket, sleeveless sweater, a knit tie, and slacks. I was carrying *The New York Times*, a paper I had read on the train.

During a discussion on selecting jury members, one of the lawyers said, "I'd never allow Mr. Fast on one of my juries! That tweed jacket and sweater spells out 'intellectual' to me. Also the paper you're reading. I don't want any intellectual on my jury. They think too much. Now if you were carrying the *Daily News* . . ."

Picking a jury by the papers they read is not so farfetched. One lawyer I spoke to said that as a prosecutor he would strike anyone reading *The New York Times*, but perhaps accept a reader of *The Wall Street Journal*. "Tabloids or trash novels are okay, but forget anyone carrying *War and Peace* into the courtroom!"

What a person reads as well as how he or she dresses projects a subtext. A subtext can be read into almost any part of a person. An African-American trial lawyer I talked to said he uses his color and minority status as a positive image. "People still have biases about a person's color. They don't have huge expectations for me, and I throw them off base by being bright and articulate. Whatever I do or say then seems a bit better."

Another lawyer, a Vietnam veteran with one leg, told me that he refused to use a prosthesis. "I come to the courtroom early and put my crutches below the table. At a crucial moment I will stand up, holding the table, and make my point. The jury suddenly sees my disability. What theater! What a subtext I send out! Believe me, it always works."

However, I was told of a lawyer with a flamboyant style who favors white suits and suspenders and gets away with it—but only because he has the panache to carry it off, and because he is an extremely clever man. The subtext he projects is suitable to his style and delivery and to the court in which he operates. The same clothes on another man could be laughable and a disaster. The subtext must suit the style. In general, men are best advised to avoid slacks and sport jackets and stick to suits.

For women in law, subdued colors are best, if the image is to be serious. As the shades of color lighten, the subtext that a woman projects lightens as well. A softer image is projected by beiges and browns. A woman can wear a suit, as most women lawyers do, but she can also go for a smart dress or a skirt and blouse in court, being always conscious of the subtext she wishes to project.

Again, there are exceptions. A young lawyer from Marin County in California told me that she once dared to go into court in jeans. "The judge gave me some flack, but not much. I knew he had jeans on under his robes. It was the jury I wanted to reach. They were all young, counterculture types, and I knew they'd react negatively to the subtext sent by a suit or even a dress. I know the jeans swung the case in my favor." This approach would be foolish in most cases, but this time it worked to project an image with which the jury could identify.

The subtext the jury perceives is often a determining factor in a case. In a rape trial, for example, verdicts often depend not on the facts, but on the appearance, reputation, social life, and demeanor of the accused—in short, on his subtext!

According to Dr. Barbara F. Reskin, a professor of sociology at the University of Michigan, jurors tend to place the accused in a rape case in two categories. If he seems a loser, disheveled, unemployed, and unmarried, jurors are biased against him. But if he is good-looking and has a girlfriend or is married, the jurors usually do not believe he would commit rape. "He doesn't look like a rapist," was often heard. Most men and more than half of women jurors surveyed had this attitude.

In the courtroom, lawyers are faced with a particular problem— jurors who tend to accept the subtext projected by the image of the man or woman on trial. Attractive people are favored by most jurors. Well-dressed people are seen as less likely to be guilty.

It's standard procedure for a lawyer to dress petty criminals in sober attire, to groom their hair, dress them in a shirt and tie, and even give them spectacles for a scholarly look.

Cleanliness may not be next to godliness, but it is tremendously important for the man or woman on trial. There is an ingrained belief in most jurors' minds that someone who keeps clean, no matter what class he or she comes from, is inherently decent—a subtext that every lawyer should wish a jury to perceive in a client. Defendants are advised to create a subtext of good citizenship.

CHANGE THE IMAGE:
CHANGE THE SUBTEXT

Recently, Donny Osmond, the sweet Mormon boy who nearly twenty years ago charmed the nation with his song "Puppy Love," and who was held up as a role model for youngsters because of his healthy, clean-cut subtext, decided to make a change. Saccharine sentimentality is out now, and pop roughness is in. The new Osmond has a ragged haircut, wears a black leather jacket, a work shirt, worn jeans, and boots. He sings "Soldier of Love" now to a strong beat. The subtext? A brooding, repressed violence meant to appeal to today's youth market.

Has Donny changed, or is it only his subtext that has changed? Dr. Barry Schlenker, a social psychologist at the University of Florida, says, "Our identities . . . are something we have constructed with the help and agreement of others. If Osmond wears a leather jacket, we say, 'Why would a nice, sweet guy like him wear that jacket?' "

But is Osmond a nice, sweet guy inside? Which is real and

which is the image? Donny, who for years has symbolized whole-someness and Mom's apple pie, says what we see now, the sophisticated person, is what he's been all along. He claims that the audience has misperceived what he was.

If we can believe that, we can also believe in the Tooth Fairy. Images and the subtexts change because the audience wants that change. Entertainers like Osmond are well aware of the importance of image in creating a subtext. They also know that the subtext they create clings to them. The audience usually believes that the role matches the performer's personality. They believe that the subtext is real.

In the workplace, you can apply the truths learned by entertainers, politicians, television executives, and others in the business of image projection. Sometimes the clothes—and hair, and facial expression—do make the man. Simon Jones, the well-known English actor who appeared as Bridie in "Brideshead Revisited," noted that during the filming of the series the crew "tended to treat the actors who were playing aristocrats with far greater respect than those playing servants." He also has noticed that "if you're playing a clergyman, the cast and crew have a tendency to avoid swearing."

ALL THE WORLD'S A STAGE

A strong link exists between your ability to "act" a certain way and the subtext you send out to the world. A successful businessman told me, "I choose my clothes each day depending on the way I feel. When I'm low, for one reason or another, and I feel I'm going to have a hard of a time of it, I'll wear something upbeat, a tie with a little life to it, one of my brighter shirts. I try to perk up my image."

When I pressed him about this, he said, "It's not so much to change the way I feel as it is to convince everyone else that I'm really dealing with things. The trouble is, no matter how I dress, it's not too hard for people to read me, to see the subtext, 'I can't handle things today!' Thank God it doesn't happen often."

Another friend, the director of a national foundation, says she faces the same problem. "There are times when I simply can't cope with things, and usually they are the exact times I don't want the people who work for me to know I can't manage."

"What do you do?"

She shrugged. "I become someone else. If I have a meeting and I want to look very efficient, I decide I'll be a Sigourney Weaver type. That takes a smart suit and a beautiful blouse and pin. If I have to coax a donation out of a big shot, I'll be Blanche DuBois with a few ruffles, and if I go from the office right to someone's house for dinner, I can be Doris Day. I use pretenses to send out a particular image."

Selecting an image and trying to live up to it may not help much in actually dealing with the problem at hand, but it could send out a subtext that you are dealing just fine, thereby gaining the confidence of those around you. Still, there are better ways. While playacting can work for some, other methods are necessary for people who often have problems dealing with situations, and therefore send out a subtext of inadequacy.

Today's world is an overwhelming one, and many people find it difficult and often impossible to handle the economic and political upheavals of our time, the turmoil of our troubled cities—and, on a more intimate level, the difficulties of the workplace or personal life.

All these problems create anxieties which we may often feel helpless to handle. Others then sense a subtext of helplessness in us. So, it is important to reduce the anxieties, to deal realistically with life, and change the subtext that others read in us.

Each of us is different, thus each has a different method of coping with life. We all, however, use certain basic external techniques. Learning, understanding, and using these techniques will allow us to manage life better and control the subtext we send out to others, changing the way others see us and enabling us to successfully handle our jobs and make our way up the corporate ladder.

2

SUPERTALK

THE MAN WITH SOMETHING MISSING

"When I hired Mark," Ed told me, "I really thought that he was the man for the job. I needed someone who could handle the clients, who knew the business."

Ed's brokerage firm was in trouble, and he was using me as a sounding board to discuss his problems. "Has Mark worked out?" I asked.

"Well, that's the trouble." Ed shook his head. "I can't be sure.

"He's popular with the clients, and that's half the battle, but the other half is doing the job, and unfortunately that's where there's something missing. The man has no business sense!"

I didn't understand what Ed meant until I met Mark, and then it became clear. I liked him instantly. He was tall, well built, with a youthful face and stylish gray sideburns, and he had an easy and comfortable style. And his voice! It was deep and resonant. Its low register signaled strength, determination, and serenity. You couldn't help but trust a man like Mark.

"What you have," I told Ed later, "is a contradiction between Mark's subtext and his abilities. You say he can't do the job, but my God, he comes on strong. That voice is reassuring, sincere, a definite asset."

"And the clients love him. What can I do?"

I thought about it for a moment, then shrugged. "Use him where he's strongest. Make him part of a team where the other man or woman can do the job but doesn't impress the client. Maybe by working with a competent partner he'll realize what's expected."

"In other words, I pay two people to do one job."

"Is it worth it?"

"I'll have to think it over," Ed told me, but a few weeks later he confessed that he had let Mark go. "If only he knew the score— but I'm sure he'll have no trouble getting another job and holding it until the boss catches on. You know, he's taught me a lesson. Looks and charm work for a while, but they can't compare with doing the job right!"

RESONANCE, REGISTER, AND PITCH

Our voices and how we use them send out very strong subtextual messages. By manipulating the resonance and register of his voice,

Mark was able to project a subtext of dependability and success. It is this subtext that makes us trust certain television personalities. Walter Cronkite is the best example: The low pitch and resonance of his voice signal honesty and believability.

In the motion picture *Broadcast News*, the plot hinged on a contradiction between subtext and ability. William Hurt played a newscaster whose intelligence and understanding of events was limited, but whose resonant, authoritative voice and empathetic manner came across very successfully on the screen. Teamed up with a reporter who was both intelligent and capable, he managed to rise to prominence as an anchorman. His success was due to his instinctive ability to effectively harness the subtext of his voice and manner.

In television newscasting, a lower pitch and a deep resonance are most desirable. High-pitched voices present a subtext of ineffectiveness no matter how capable and able the person is.

Women like Mariette Hartley are blessed by nature with the low pitch and register that come across so well. However, Hartley's failure on a morning news show makes it clear that a strong voice alone cannot guarantee success in that field.

Pitch, resonance, and register are three of the most important elements in conveying subtext through the voice. To define them briefly: *Pitch* is the highness or lowness of a sound; *resonance* is the vibration given the voice by the vocal chambers such as the mouth or pharynx; and *register* is the range of the voice.

Many of us can, to an extent, control these elements. We can resonate through the chest to signal strength, dependability, firmness, solidity. An authoritative voice resonates from the chest. The extent to which you control your register depends upon your vocal cords. If they are thin and tight, and you resonate through the head, your voice will be high and delicate. Heavy cords and a good, strong chest can give deep, mellow, earthy tones.

Pitch, too, is dependent on the vocal cords. We tighten our cords to raise our pitch and convey a subtext of anger, fear, or joy. When we are depressed or very tired, our vocal cords lose their tension, and our pitch is lowered. While a low pitch can help to transmit confidence and sincerity, it can also convey a subtext of depression and weariness—and, paradoxically, one of sexuality. Marlene Dietrich provides a classic example of how low pitch and a husky register can signal a seductive subtext.

THE MELODY LINGERS ON

Another important part of the subtext of speech is a rather elusive quality called melody, which is the rhythm, music, and harmony of speech. A friend told me how he used melody to enjoy a season of rich, classical music. When he was a young man growing up in Cleveland, he longed to attend the concerts at Severance Hall, but he couldn't afford the admission fee. He and a friend bought secondhand tuxedos at a thrift shop and each concert night they walked to the backstage entrance, talking to each other in agitated Russian. They would wave aside the bewildered doorman, who assumed they were foreign members of the orchestra, then go through the stage door down to the floor and find empty seats.

The point is that neither one could really speak a word of Russian. "How did you do it?" I asked.

"Well"—my friend shrugged—"the doorman didn't know Russian either, so we used nonsense words that sounded like Russian, and we were good mimics, so we were able to catch the melody of the language."

It is that melody that stand-up comics sometimes use while talking gobbledygook and making it sound like a foreign language. Sid Caesar is magnificent at this.

Every language and every dialect of a language has its own melody, which is affected by grammatical structure, emotional content, mood, and attitude—and every melody has a subtext of its own. In addition to the rhythm, music, and harmony, melody incorporates pitch, register, resonance, speed, and volume.

When you change the melody in your voice, you change the subtext of what you say. In a job interview a simple statement, such as "I'd like to work here" can ring with conviction if the melody is right or fall flat as a pancake if there is no melody to it. Try saying it in as many ways as you can, and you'll realize what melody is all about.

A "detail man" I worked with in a pharmaceutical company used to complain about the difficulty he had with doctors. "I hardly get into my sales pitch before they tune out. They say, 'I've got patients waiting. Leave the samples and literature.' But I know that they give detail men from other houses a lot of time!"

What was wrong with this salesman was a flat, expressionless voice, one that lacked melody. It had a subtext of weariness and boredom. Whether he meant it or not, his voice sent the message "This is my job. It's dull and uninteresting. I couldn't care less if you listened to me."

When I got to know him better, I found that he came from a family where any display of emotion was considered "common," and this attitude must have rubbed off on him. He was simply behaving in a way he had always behaved, not realizing how it affected him professionally.

THE POWER OF LOUD

Several years ago, I was an observer at a sales seminar. It had been in progress for most of the day and the attendees were exhausted, dispirited, and fed up with the slogans and suggestions they had been given.

Sensing this, the leader suddenly took a new tack. "Are you going to make that sale?" he yelled out suddenly.

Bewildered, the salespeople responded with halfhearted yeses.

Again, he yelled out, "Let me hear it! Stronger! I'll make that sale!"

The answer was a little louder, and again he thundered out, "I'll make that sale!" His volume was up and his voice booming.

It was as if a charge of electricity had galvanized the audience. Suddenly their tiredness slipped away as they began to match his volume. I'll make that sale! I'll make that sale! The room rocked with their enthusiasm, and later, leaving the hall, I heard them talking in excited voices: "What a session!" "Dynamite!" "He really got the juices flowing!"

What had happened to change a tired group into such an eager bunch? Subtext. The message behind the booming shout of the leader was sheer power. By matching their volume to his, they had also matched his subtext and had felt an infusion of energy at the end of an exhausting day.

While raising the volume of your voice can emphasize what you are saying in casual conversation and add a subtext of power and strength, lowering the voice can also achieve the same subtext. I once worked for a CEO who, at staff meetings, would deliberately lower his voice to push home significant facts. We had to lean forward to hear him—and we did because we knew and understood the subtext of that lowered voice: "I'm in power here. Hear what I say the first time, or you might not be around the second time!"

THE PHONINESS OF FAST TALK

"He almost had me sold," Kurt told me as we left the secondhand auto dealership. "I liked the car and the test drive was okay. I guessed he sensed that my initial doubts were wearing off, because suddenly he began to 'fast talk' me. I got suspicious right away and figured he was trying to con me!"

What we call "fast talk" is talk we sense as false. The subtext is obvious: I'll say anything to get you to do what I want, whether it's true or not. What is less obvious is just how much actual speed or slowness of speech conveys in terms of subtext. Fast talk may actually signal a "con" job. Or sometimes, a speeding up of words can signal embarrassment or awkwardness. Nancy, complaining to her office manager about an incident she perceived as sexual harassment, begins to rush her words together, so much so that the office manager can barely understand her. However, her subtext of awkwardness and shame comes through clearly. Conversely, the moderately slow talker often conveys a subtext of conviction, thoughtfulness, interest, and sincerity.

A ROSE BY ANY OTHER NAME

Some time ago, Los Angeles economist Arthur H. Hawkins wrote an article on labor-management relations. The gist of the article was that certain terms or labels we use call up inaccurate subtexts. Why not change the labels and thus change the subtext? For example, labor has a historical overtone of manual toil. Most people we think of as laborers have nothing to do with toil, however. Hawkins suggested we call them the paycheck population.

He would have us make a few other changes as well. *Cease to purchase* could substitute for *boycott; motivation through fear* for *coercion; difference* for *dispute; temporary work cessation* for *layoff.* For *segregation,* why not use *distinction without evaluation?* For *scab,* how about *noncertified worker?*

Hawkins's recommendations clearly align with management's thinking. The words *scab, segregation, boycott,* and the others call up a very strong subtext. Labor, or the paycheck population, has used them for years to make a point. They are welded to uneasiness in our collective consciousness. They arouse a definite, almost palpable, subtext and certainly changing them would destroy that subtext. Do we, as a culture, want that?

Euphemisms, the use of one word for another to create a more favorable subtext, is nothing new. People in the Victorian era were adept at it. Even the word *legs* brought to mind too sexual a subtext for them. *Limbs* were gentler, more delicate. We accept more today, but we still don't like the subtext behind *died.* Friends and relatives *pass away* or *pass over.* She *left us,* he's *gone.*

In business, euphemisms, along with jargon and slang, create a subtext of inside knowledge. Tune in on Harper, the CEO of a middle-sized company, talking to his new marketing people. "It wouldn't hurt you to interact with some of the competition (find out what the competition is up to). When that deal fell through you just didn't see the right *button pusher* (decision maker). And, Jim, you're the man for junk bonds. I don't want anyone else treading on Jim's turf. (Here's slang for "field of exploitation" borrowed directly from street gangs. It may, subtextually, give a hint of the ruthlessness of wheeling and dealing in the marketplace.)

And finally," Harper winds up, "Gary, you've been evaluating that new outfit, Cooperative Ratchets. Tell me about their R's." (Here's jargon used to cover ROE—return on equity; ROA—return on account; and ROI—return on investments. Lumping these together under the term "R's" gives a subtext of a CEO in a hurry, a CEO who hasn't time to fool around, a CEO after facts and performance. It impresses the marketing people!)

Words—what they mean, what they express, and how we use them—are very much the basic stuff of verbal subtext. We call someone skinny, and it's a derogatory description. We call that same person slim, and it's a compliment. We can make a list of words that have the same meaning but arouse different subtexts, some positive, some negative. Just think, do we compliment the boss or flatter him? Is a fellow worker stubborn, or someone with perseverance? Is the personnel director selective, or is she picky? Is the office Romeo suave or just glib?

In any discussion, the words we choose to label people can create a positive or negative subtext. The clever speaker uses words with discrimination and deliberation.

A QUICK COURSE IN SPEAKING

What can we learn from this chapter about either public speaking or private speaking? One important point is to begin to study and analyze your own voice. Does it reflect what you want to say, or does the subtext behind your words contradict the text you use? Use role models whose subtexts you admire. Analyze their voices for all the different qualities and try to apply those qualities to your own speech.

The first thing to do is hear yourself as others hear you. Nobody can be objective about his or her own voice. You must distance yourself from your voice, and the best way to do this is by using a tape recording with excellent fidelity. It is worth the investment of buying or renting equipment.

Set up imaginary situations, such as buying, selling, talking to the boss, talking to subordinates—then tape yourself in these situations. Let a week or so go by between taping and listening to the tape. Then listen analytically. Is your voice too high? Too low? Is the pitch right? The resonance? The register? The speed? The pausing? Do you use too many fillers like "uh" or "I mean" or "you know" or the current favorite, "basically"?

I was once a guest on a radio talk show, and tacked to the wall of the studio a large sign warned that "I mean," "uh," and "you know" could take up more than 50 percent of precious air time. Fillers like these can waste time in any tight situation, not to mention sending out a subtext of indecision and uncertainty. Clear thinkers—at least those who want others to perceive them as clear thinkers—speak clearly.

Most important, does your voice reflect what you want to say? Is your subtext in tune with your text? Is there any quality in your voice that will turn people off?

Once you've picked up what's wrong with your voice, decide what changes you want. Experiment with your voice on tape and keep playing it back until it pleases you.

3

TOUCHY
SITUATIONS

THE ART OF SHAKING HANDS

Of all the elements that make up a person's subtext, none is as intimate as touch. If it is used correctly, touch can overcome barriers, dissolve anger, and create a feeling of trust and warmth. Used unwisely, it can put up barriers, cause annoyance and anger, and betray both trust and confidence.

In any business situation, the first possibility of touch comes with the handshake. It is the first step on meeting a new person or greeting an old friend, an associate, or even an antagonist. The hands come together, and the subtext of their union tells us a great deal about the person we are dealing with.

A limp handshake always sends a subtext of disinterest. The handshake that offers only the front half of the fingers says, "I don't want to become too involved with you." Particular to men is the bone-cracking "macho" shake, which sends out a subtext of aggressiveness and an eagerness to compete.

Women in the corporate world have their own concern with the handshake. It is only in recent years that they have begun to shake hands. The necessity to do so is undeniable, but a cultural reluctance still lingers on. Women who want to appear strong and competent, but not too masculine, have to relearn the entire technique of shaking hands. The old-fashioned woman's shake gave only half the hand, the fingers, and was diffident. Unfortunately, it sent out a weak and uncertain subtext.

The proper female handshake for today is one in which the entire hand is given to the shaker, and the shaker's hand is grasped in a firm but not hard shake. The hand is then released, but not too promptly. The subtext is competence and control.

Too prompt a release sends a message of not wishing to get involved. Between two men, holding the hand for a longer time, four or five seconds, sends a subtext of I like you. Between a woman and a man, too long a period of holding the shake signals a subtext of personal, even sexual, interest.

So, the handshaker, man or woman, must learn to follow a middle course—not too hard, not too flabby, not too long, not too short.

THE TOUCH THAT SELLS

A fascinating study gives us a clue to how the subtext of trust works. In a large library, a group of sociology students set up an experiment. They had a librarian touch the first hundred readers as they checked out books. The touch was a light one, a brush of the librarian's hand against the borrower's. Sometimes it was barely noticed.

With the next hundred readers, the librarian was told to avoid touching them, to make no physical contact. Otherwise the procedure was the same. The librarian gave the exact same service to both groups.

Researchers stationed outside the library approached each reader as he or she left and explained that they were conducting a study of library service, and asked each reader to answer a few questions about the library. Buried among the questions was one that asked how willing and helpful the librarian had been. Among those who had been touched, the great majority described the librarian as helpful and considerate. The readers who had not been touched had neither positive nor negative feelings about the librarian.

This is not an isolated finding. Another telling clue to the importance of touch came from some informal reporting by the owner of a car dealership. He noticed that one of his salespeople had an unusually high record of sales. The owner watched him in action but could find nothing radically different in his approach. It was very much like the other salespeople's except that at one point in his pitch he touched the customer. The owner, by instructing the rest of the sales force to copy this technique, was able to improve sales significantly. The subtext the salesperson gave out with his touch was one of caring. The skin is our largest sense organ, and we respond emotionally when it is touched.

But as potent as touch is in selling, it also carries an innate danger. The wrong kind of touch or touching someone at the wrong time can destroy trust. With any touch that lingers too long, is heavy-handed, or seems inappropriate, the immediate question is "What did that mean?"

The successful salesperson's touch was to the upper arm or on the upper back, but it was brief, and, most important, it came at the right moment, just as the customer was half-convinced. A touch too soon, or too heavy, or in the wrong place can be devastating.

THE EXPECTED AND THE UNEXPECTED TOUCH

In his book *The Hidden Dimension*, anthropologist Dr. Edward T. Hall says that the ability to respond to touch is one of the basic criteria of life. Dr. Hall believes that one of the reasons that many Americans favor small, foreign cars is the sense the cars give of being in touch with the road.

One interpretation of touch depends on a number of different factors; one is love. We allow our loved ones to touch us; in fact, we welcome their touch because the subtext is affection. Children deprived of touch cannot develop properly, cannot learn to respond to love and affection. The closer we feel to someone, the more readily we allow that person's touch, and the warmer the subtext of that touch. This is an expected subtext. We expect love and affection from our close friends and family, and because we expect it the subtext is comforting but not too intense.

The touch of a stranger, however, since it *is* unexpected, may send a different subtext. The librarian and the salesperson mentioned earlier sent a strong, subtextual message: "Even though I don't know you, I like you." Part of those subtexts was the fleeting quality of both touches. Touching needn't be intrusive to be meaningful. In fact, had the salesperson touched the customer at the wrong moment, the entire deal could have been blown. In any business situation, touch can play an important part, either positive or negative. You must know when to touch and how to touch.

THE RULES OF THE GAME

A point to remember is that there is a strong sexual implication behind touching. While the touch of a salesperson can project a subtext of trust, in a different situation it may project harassment and sexual intrusion. A brief touch of the hand on a shoulder, or even an arm casually placed around a shoulder is acceptable in business, provided it is man-to-man. If a man touches a woman, the touch must be lighter, briefer, and less intrusive than an arm around the shoulder. There is the ever-present sexual subtext in any relationship between men and women. This subtext can be devastating—or useful, depending on many factors.

There is a hierarchy to touching. While a man touching a woman must do it briefly and lightly, a woman touching a man can hold the touch longer. It can be heavier, but the woman, too, must be aware of the sexual subtext.

The right to touch someone in our society is largely determined by status. Someone of higher status may touch someone of lower status. The president may touch the CEO, the CEO may touch the lower executive, the executives may touch the workers. The secretary may not touch the executive—unless they have worked together for a long time and there is an easy companionship between them.

A doctor may place an arm around the patient's shoulder as he breaks the bad or good news, but the patient usually does not touch the doctor. A lawyer may touch a client, but it is difficult for a client to touch a lawyer.

It all boils down to status. People who are richer, older, or higher on the corporate ladder may acceptably touch those who are poorer, younger, or subordinate. Children are reluctant to touch adults they don't know, but adults may touch children. Adults must be careful, however, not to assume an inappropriate familiarity with children they don't know. Respect children's needs for personal space.

Equals may touch each other. Some years ago, during the Camp David peace talks between Egypt and Israel with President Carter mediating, Anwar Sadat frequently put his hand on Carter's knee. The subtext of the gesture was warm friendship, but there was also a subtler subtext, an announcement to the world that Sadat was Carter's equal.

This brings up the question of where to touch. To Sadat, touching the knee was culturally appropriate. In the United States, a forearm can be touched with impunity, but a knee or a thigh is a different story. Sometimes a woman, touching a man's thigh as they sit talking, can send a subtext of concern. At other times it can become a sexual advance. A man touching a woman's thigh in the same situation almost always sends a sexual subtext.

THE ULTIMATE TOUCH

In spite of the care we must take in touching, we are, in many ways, a society starved for the subtext that touching sends. The love-ins and the awareness and encounter sessions of the sixties awakened a touch-starved population to the importance of touch. But the pendulum swung back in the eighties, and now in the closing years of the century we miss that easy touching. We run the risk of becoming touch starved again, and the subtext of touch becomes even more important in any relationship.

People who experience massage for the first time often overreact. They attribute much more meaning to it than it actually has. But still, it is, in a way, the ultimate touch. As beneficial as it may be to the muscles, it is even more so to the mind. We prosper from our psychological reaction to the massager's hands.

I witnessed how moving touch can be when I was teaching at the New School for Social Research in New York City. An older student, a parole officer in the New York City Correction System, described the incident.

"One of my parolees had been convicted of molesting a child. It was about the fifth time we met. We got together at a coffee shop, and I was satisfied that he was keeping his nose clean. Then, as we left, I put my arm around his shoulder.

"To my surprise and embarrassment, he broke down and began to cry. When he had pulled himself together, he told me that this was the first time since he had been convicted that anyone had touched him. It opened the floodgates!"

Sometimes touch can open the floodgates, as it did in this case, and at other times it can break down resistance. A story told to me by a young Chicago lawyer bears this out. She had a young woman for a client, a woman who had been accused of shoplifting. Getting this client to give any information about the incident was very difficult. Guilt, shame, and fear combined to keep her silent.

"I was convinced that if she could tell me her entire story, I could help her. Obviously she was withholding important information because she wasn't sure of me.

"A partner of mine who had come into the library where we were talking drew me aside and said, 'I think I know what your problem is. You're talking to her from three feet away, across the table. Look, take a chair on her side of the table and for God's sake, relax. You're too uptight!'

"I did what he suggested, and there was still no change in my client. Then, at one point, I was so intent on what I was saying that I leaned forward and put my hand on hers. Well! What a difference! She looked up at me for the first time and met my eyes. Then she began talking, and it was just what I needed to hear."

THE CULTURAL CONNECTION

Whatever subtext touching can induce, we must remember that there is a cultural connection to the practice of touch. Some cultures favor it; others seem to avoid touching as much as possible. The English and Germans are considered poor touchers, while the Spanish, Italians, Israelis, and Arabs have always seemed to savor touching. There are cultures in which touching is a very important part of communication. For example, a great deal of touching goes on during any conversation in the Middle East.

This culturally based reluctance or desire to touch can change as the society evolves. Italian men used to walk through the streets holding hands, but just a few years ago Roger Youman, an editor at *TV Guide*, visited Italy and in an article in *The New York Times Magazine* commented that you don't see men holding hands in Italy anymore.

Children still do. Italian women hold hands, link arms, or walk with arms around each other. But "Italian men rarely do so, very rarely!" Youman noted. "Something has been lost, something Italian men had that was worth saving, the ability and the freedom to express an emotional bond in unself-conscious and sexually neutral terms."

The reason, he suggests, is the increased visibility of homosexual men and the amplified homophobic attitudes of "straight" men. This may be true, and yes, I agree with Youman that something has been lost—the subtext of enormous comfort and caring in hand holding.

In the United States our culture forbids hand holding between men. Men are reluctant to touch one another, and for that reason, when they do, it is all the more intense and effective. When men are deeply troubled or in great pain, touching, holding a hand, or embracing someone can work wonders.

READING IT OUT

We all start life with a tremendous need for touch and its subtext. Babies need the touch of their mother, the feel of the nipple as they nurse, the touch of anything they can bring to their mouths.

This need for touch in our society fades a bit at the age of five or six, but it returns at puberty, a time when its subtext is sexually dangerous. Because of this "danger," society teaches pubescent girls that touch is not allowed when it comes from the other sex, but society permits them to hold hands with each other, to walk with their arms around each other and engage in same-sex touching. The wrestling of teenage boys and the contact sports they delight in take care of some of their need for touch.

Once we become adults, there is still a need to touch, although in this country it doesn't seem obvious. But the need and its practice are there. Dr. Erving Goffman, a sociologist, points this out in his book *Relations in Public Places*. "The theory that American middle class people don't touch each other when they talk is nonsense. People are handling each other all the time, but we read it out. You've got to keep your eyes open to see it."

We "read it out" because it occurs in very natural episodes. Someone squeezes past someone else in a narrow passage and takes that person's arm to get by without body contact. In conversation, one person may touch another to stop a sentence or to allow a point to be made. People touch their friends and family constantly, but lightly, and they "read out" the touch because it is so fleeting as to be subliminal.

It is intriguing that even these light touches can supply a subtext of caring and concern. And it is even more so with a stronger, longer touch—always provided the touch is appropriate in place and time.

4

BODY LANGUAGE:
THE EYES, THE HEAD,
AND THE HANDS

THE MAN WHO LISTENED

Some years ago I worked as a medical journalist for a large publication. The best part of the job was our editor-in-chief, a small, feisty man who somehow evoked a stubborn loyalty in everyone who worked for him.

At one point he had to deliver a talk to a group of students, and he asked me to videotape it for him. "I want to show my wife and kids. They'll get a kick out of it."

I taped his talk, and I was amazed at the way he charmed his audience of would-be medical writers. What was there about this insignificant-looking guy that captivated everyone? Trying to discover a pattern in his approach, I ran the tape through a few times, then played it at fast forward. Suddenly I noticed something I had missed. From the minute he mounted the podium, his head went from side to side like the tail of a friendly dog. Watching closely, I noticed that he constantly maintained eye contact with everyone in the audience, never favoring just one side, his eyes sweeping that group of students like the beam of a lighthouse.

Eye contact, I realized, was the secret of his charm. Whether he talked to one person, to a dozen, or to a roomful, he managed to make eye contact, and though he broke it, he returned to it. Conversely, when you talked to him, eye contact let you know he was listening.

Years later, when I had to lecture myself, I tried to copy that same technique, sweeping the room with my eyes to make contact with everyone I could. One time, when I was asked to talk to a group of businessmen at Xerox, I broke my glasses the day before the speech. I went to an optometrist whose sign promised GLASSES IN ONE HOUR. He took my broken glasses and shook his head. "These are bifocals. Reading glasses I can give you in an hour, or distance glasses, but not bifocals. That'll take a week!"

What a dilemma. With reading glasses I could see my notes, but not the eyes of the audience. With distance glasses I couldn't see my notes, but I could see the eyes of the audience. Which to choose? In the end I opted for the distance glasses. I could always memorize the notes, but to avoid eye contact during the speech would be deadly. I'd send out a subtext of coldness and withdrawal.

THE TWO-AND-A-HALF-BILLION-DOLLAR VERDICT

Of all the elements we use to communicate with other people, eye contact is the most important—and the most human. Animals are disturbed by eye contact. To them, it carries a subtext of threat. Humans are pleased with it. To them the subtexts are attention and interest.

The importance of the subtext sent by eye contact was evident in a lawsuit that took place between two oil companies a while back. Pennzoil sued Texaco, claiming that Texaco had improperly interfered with a deal it had with Getty Oil. Pennzoil won a damage award of over two and a half billion dollars plus interest, the largest in the history of the United States.

During the trial, the Texaco lawyers thought Pennzoil's counsel were playing up to the jury by instructing their witnesses always to make eye contact with the jurors and to joke with them.

In an attempt to paint a contrast, Texaco counsel instructed their witnesses to be serious and absolutely avoid looking at the jurors. The case went against Texaco, and in conversations after the verdict, the jurors said, "Those Texaco witnesses never looked at us once. They were arrogant and indifferent. How could we believe them?"

Conventional legal wisdom says Texaco counsel were right in "not putting on a show for the jury." But their witnesses were so concerned with avoiding eye contact that they sent out a subtext of insincerity, the very thing the lawyers were trying to avoid!

If anyone were to doubt the strength of the subtext behind eye contact, a statement from an Israeli Army officer should put that doubt to rest. Lieutenant Colonel Ysrael of the occupied West Bank told *The New York Times* that on most days he and his men face a battle of eyes, Israeli eyes against Palestinian eyes, looks meant to kill against glances meant to intimidate, darting glances against blank stares, eyes begging for a little friendship meeting eyes round with fear. It is what the soldiers call "the war of the eyes."

The most piercing and chilling looks come from the Palestinian teenagers, according to Colonel Ysrael. "Even if you give them a daring, intimidating look, they stare right back at you with self-confidence. Their parents are different. You feel that you can negotiate with their eyes. The eyes say you can even shake my hand."

The most interesting looks come from the Arab girls, according to another soldier, Lieutenant Eldad, a twenty-three-year-old. "They are very interested. They tease you, but they are embarrassed."

What a world of emotions expressed only with the eyes!

THE RULES OF THE GAME

There are definite rules for eye contact. There is what one sociologist has called "the moral looking time," the length of time you can hold eye contact with a stranger without sending a particular message or offending or disturbing that person. Making eye contact for too long a period can be disconcerting, even threatening. The subtext of caring and interest becomes distorted.

However, failing to make eye contact sends the disturbing subtext

"I do not meet your eye because to me you are not there, you are a nonperson, insignificant."

Understanding this, we can realize that an important subtext of eye contact is recognition. If you encounter a panhandler in the street, refusing to meet his eyes says, "I do not recognize your existence." If you do make eye contact, you leave yourself vulnerable to the panhandler's approach. This is so ingrained a reaction that I have seen people avoiding eye contact with a blind beggar!

Refusing to make eye contact can also send a subtext of arrogance and contempt. It says, "I am better than you," and we reserve it not only for panhandlers but also for servants and employees in certain circumstances. The boss will frequently avoid eye contact with one of his workers, a foolish move because of the insulting message sent out.

The "moral looking time" is different in different places. In an elevator, it hardly exists. If you make eye contact with a stranger, you break it at once, you look ahead, up at the floor numbers or down at the floor—anywhere but in another's eyes. In a room, the moral looking time is longer. You can make eye contact and hold it for two or three seconds, but then, for comfort, you must break it. Extended eye contact between the sexes or between two women usually means "I am interested in you." Between two men who do not know each other, the longer eye contact usually has a threatening subtext.

In a large room like a boardroom or a lecture hall, the speaker can make eye contact with people in the audience and hold it as long as he or she wishes. But on the street, the "moral looking time" is very short. Any glance longer than a brief, sweeping one becomes a sign of recognition with the subtext "Do I know you?" Held too long, it sends a subtext of rudeness. Combined with a brief smile and a nod, however, the rudeness disappears. In many such encounters there is a moment of embarrassment when you realize that eye contact has been too long because one or the other has allowed it. The smile or nod or even a quick hello eases the situation.

I remember attending a convention in Chicago and wandering about the convention hall examining the exhibits. At one point I noticed an exceptionally well dressed middle-aged man with striking white hair and a very deep tan. He looked every inch the top executive, and forgetting myself I stared at him.

He caught my eye and hesitated momentarily as I smiled. Then, rather than break eye contact, he smiled back at me and, as we approached each other, he put out his hand. We shook hands, and he asked how I was, how the job was going, and a few other generalized questions. Then, with a smile, said, "Let's get together for lunch soon" and walked off. My prolonged staring and eye contact combined with my smile had sent a subtext of "I know you." Rather than risk offending a potentially useful contact, he had pretended recognition.

Of course, these are the rules for eye contact between strangers. Between friends or acquaintances eye contact can be prolonged within an appropriate comfort level. Held for too long, eye contact transmits uneasiness. Eye contact in a business setting signals trust and sincerity, as long as it is not prolonged. The proper method is to break eye contact frequently as you talk or listen. The best technique is to look down to the side, and then back.

Remember, though, that the rules of eye contact vary from culture to culture. In our culture, prolonged eye contact is too disturbing, just as a refusal to make eye contact arouses suspicion. In other cultures, particularly many Latin American ones, eye contact is linked to status. Workers keep their eyes averted when they are talking to the boss. In the States, workers can look the boss in the eye unflinchingly.

Some societies favor prolonged eye contact and are uneasy when it is broken too soon. I once had some dealings with a young Liberian businessman who worked for Firestone. He was very angry with an executive in my company who was trying to firm up a deal with him. "I don't trust that man!" he told me.

"He's very honest and sincere," I protested.

The Liberian shook his head. "He doesn't keep looking me in the eye."

I began to see the light. "In this country, we feel it's rude to keep staring into someone's eyes," I tried to explain.

He brushed my explanation aside. "In my country you look a person straight in the eye as long as you talk to him. Anything else is dishonest!"

I don't think I ever convinced him that the executive was an honest man, and by the end of our talk he was beginning to doubt me. Such was the power of his own cultural upbringing.

STONEWALLING IT

When I was teaching nonverbal communication, a young man in one of my classes came to me after class and said, "I've got a real problem in communication. Maybe you can help me."

I asked what the problem was, and he said, "It's at work. I'll talk to a customer, and I know I'm saying everything right, but after a while it's as if a stone wall comes up between us. He'll just turn off.

"And it's not only work. I'm single, and I hang out at the bars pretty often. I know what you've said about eye contact, and I can look over the women in the bar and realize that the ones who let me make eye contact for longer than the 'moral looking time' are the ones who are interested in meeting me. But after talking to them for a few minutes, that same thing happens—the feeling of butting against a stone wall!"

Talking to him, it became obvious what that "stone wall" was. For some reason he had never learned one of the decisive subtextual signals, the head nod. He would talk and listen without ever moving his head.

The head nod is tremendously important in communication. I tell you something, and you nod as I say it. That nod sends a subtext of "Yes, I understand." You talk back to me, and I nod again, sending the "Yes, I understand" signal along with "I agree."

These gestures, along with the negative head shake, usually accompany all conversations and are vital to communication. The head nod, in fact, is so strong that some salespeople can use it to overcome a customer's resistance, particularly if the accompanying sales pitch is correct. The nodding elicits a positive response in the listener. It is effective in sales, in the boardroom, and in any ongoing discussion or negotiation.

Not using that head nod was, in my student's words, putting up a "stone wall." Once he understood this and began to put nodding to good use, the wall came tumbling down. Of course, using the head nod properly is very important. A senseless bobbing of the head sends a senseless subtext. The nod should be used when you agree with the other person, or when you want agreement with a point you are making, or when you want to show that yes, you understand.

In public speaking or in addressing a small group, the head nods or absence of nods will tell you whether or not you are reaching your audience. A clever speaker can gauge the audience's reaction from their nods or lack of nods and can easily switch to a subject the audience may relate to more.

BODY LANGUAGE BLINDNESS

The inability to learn the body language that sends out definite subtexts is not unusual, but it can be very destructive. In adults it can lead to an inability to relate to others, and in the job world it can be downright disastrous.

Studies have shown that this type of body language blindness often starts in childhood. Ten percent of all children have problems with sending and reading subtexts. Dr. Stephen Nowicki, a psychologist at Emory University in Atlanta, says that most emotional subtexts between people are communicated nonverbally, through body language.

The inability to read or send such messages properly is a major social handicap. "Because they are unaware of the messages they are sending or misinterpret how others are feeling," Dr. Nowicki says, "unpopular children may not even realize that they are initiating many of the negative reactions they receive from their peers."

These children feel that they have no control over the way other people treat them, and eventually they can become emotionally disturbed, anxious, depressed, or angry. What is learned in childhood is carried into adult life. In business they continue to misinterpret other people's subtexts and, in turn, send out incorrect subtexts of their own.

This is the bad news. The good news is that once they do learn to interpret subtexts of others correctly and to send the messages they want, their defeatism disappears. In other words, learning the facts about subtext, nodding, eye contact, gesture, and personal space can help them relate to other people in their private life and in the workplace.

Eye contact and head nodding are two important elements in subtextual communication. Gestures are a third. The wrong gesture can confuse and annoy. At a boardroom meeting once, for example, the CEO of the company gave some good advice about dealing with the representatives of another company. "I want to finesse them on this deal, and I think we ought to use a form of quiet diplomacy."

But even as he said it, he pounded the table in front of him with his fist. The subtext of the gesture didn't match the text of his message, and we all left the room confused about what he meant. His words were placating, but the table pounding was aggressive. What did he want us to do?

This same CEO, shortly before the company went bankrupt, assured his employees that their jobs were safe, and that the company was on a firm foundation. As he talked, however, his left hand was clenched so tightly that the knuckles showed white. His employees heard his words, but they also understood the subtext of tension that his clenched fist conveyed, and the next day they all began to get their résumés together.

AUTOMATIC GESTURES

The gestures we make are sometimes deliberate, but more often they are made on an unconscious level. We are not aware of what we are doing. If we hesitate in our speech or grasp for a word, our gestures tend to become more eloquent, as if the gestures themselves are a substitute for lost words.

Ask someone to repeat something, and he or she will often add gestures that weren't there before. It's as if the gestures help you to understand—and they do. When you want someone to like you or believe what you are saying, you will tend to use more gestures, realizing, on an unconscious level, that the gestures clarify and convince.

The tight fist the CEO used under pressure was an unconscious gesture that gave away the truth. It was made without thinking, and its subtext contradicted the words he used. The same sort of unconscious gesture is the nose rub. A speaker is about to lie or make an outrageous statement, and the finger automatically strokes the nose.

These automatic gestures, just because they are made without thinking, tend to send a more honest subtext than our words. Watch a politician make campaign promises he cannot fulfill and you will usually see that unbidden nose rub. Watch an executive make predictions he knows are wrong, and the same nose rub occurs—unless, of course, the politician and the executive know about these gestures and restrain them.

Different subtexts can be sent by the same gesture, depending on whether a man or woman uses it. There are basic differences between men and women in regard to emotions and mental outlook. This doesn't mean that men are less articulate or women more emotional, nor are attributes such as aggression, intuition, gentleness, or pragmatism limited to just one sex. However, many people believe these attributes are sex-linked, and this belief affects the way they perceive the subtexts of men and women.

A woman may be brought up to believe that extravagant gestures are not feminine, and therefore it would be wrong for her to use them in a business setting. A man may be taught that it isn't manly to show emotion, and this can affect the subtext of his gestures. Still, we are reasoning creatures, and we can change our habits.

While some gestures are more prevalent among members of one sex or another (a man straightening his tie, a woman pushing back her hair), none is absolutely linked to one sex. And even though many are automatic gestures, they can still be brought into the conscious realm and made in a calculated way.

Learning to use gestures deliberately and understand their subtexts can become a powerful tool to project honesty and truth. It is a clever form of manipulation, but it must be done with subtlety.

GESTURES AND THEIR MEANING

Here is a brief summary of some of the more important gestures we use and the subtexts they send.

An open-palmed gesture with the hand moving forward at chest height, fingers up and palm out, sends a forceful subtext of seriousness and importance.

Both hands open at chest level and spread sideways, palms up, sends a subtext of helplessness, a plea to be understood.

One hand raised above the head emphasizes a point; two hands raised above the head signal triumph.

An index finger to the ear or rubbing the eye signals rejection.

A hand or fingers in front of the mouth betrays a reluctance to talk, a holding back, telling only half the story.

A placating subtext is sent with the palm up, hand out—if it is used by a man. The same gesture used by a woman has a courting or flirting subtext.

Sitting back and listening to someone while you steeple your fingers sends out a subtext of confidence. Steepling is holding the hands together at chest height with the fingers touching and pointing upward. The higher the hands are held, the stronger the subtext of confidence, but they should not go above the level of the chin.

Wagging a forefinger back and forth is a classic negative sign and sends a subtext of "You are wrong."

Pointing sends an aggressive subtext, and using an object to point with, a pen or a cigar, extends the threatening finger and makes the subtext more intrusive, more aggressive.

Another aggressive subtext is sent when you stand with your hands on your hips, your thumbs back. Here the subtext is confidence and toughness. In speech making, a subtext of confidence and logic is sent by counting things off on your fingers. It can make a presentation more forceful.

Rubbing the hands briefly (not wringing them) suggests confidence in what you are saying. Hands clasped behind the back send a subtext of "I am in charge here."

You can send a subtext of confidence and pleasure in someone else's presentation by leaning back in a chair with your fingers laced behind your head.

THE NEGATIVE SIDE

These are positive signals you can learn to help yourself or to interpret the subtexts of others. However, you should also understand the negative signals that send out a loser subtext. It is important to avoid them yourself and understand them in others.

The meaning of these gestures comes from research with videotapes taken during psychological therapy sessions. Gestures were matched against the patients' statements. As an example, a woman covered her eyes as she told of an incident she was ashamed of. The subtext behind covering the eyes became clear.

Chewing a pencil or other objects signals nervousness and uncertainty. Putting a hand over the mouth sends a subtext of embarrassment, of hiding something, or of a reluctance to speak.

Clenching or wringing the hands signals nervousness or anger. Crossing the arms over the chest sends a subtext of "I don't agree with you."

This last gesture has to be interpreted carefully. Someone may sit with crossed arms because it is a comfortable position. To interpret it as resistance, you must look for tightness and tension in the rest of the body. Some time ago Dr. Benjamin Spock spoke to a group of police officers. Dr. Spock and the police thought differently about most matters. A picture taken from the podium showed almost all the policemen sitting with crossed arms. There was no doubt about the subtext they sent out!

THE CULTURAL CONNECTION

I've mentioned that the rules for eye contact differ from society to society, but gestures are even more closely linked to culture. This linkage is so strong that a person talented in reading subtexts can usually guess what country someone is from by observing the way that person uses his or her hands.

Certain general rules apply. People from the northern countries of the Western world tend to use fewer gestures than people from the south. Scandinavians, Germans, Swiss, and English use few hand gestures. To southerners they often seem stiff and immobile. The subtext is one of standoffishness, a desire not to be involved.

In southern countries, such as France, Spain, Italy, and Greece, gestures are more open, effusive, and expressive. The subtexts are vigor and emotional involvement. Israel, Arab nations, and most Central and South American countries are also rich in hand gestures.

In the United States, the traditional melting pot, it becomes more difficult to identify ethnic types from their gestures. The rules of the old countries barely hold, and very gradually a mixture of gesture and expression that can be labeled "Made in the United States" is born.

Dr. David Efron, a researcher in gestures, analyzed a number of gestural styles and related them to different cultures. Jews, he found, tend to keep their hands close to the body when they gesticulate. Their movements are choppy and full of nervous energy, usually one handed. Italians, on the other hand, use expansive gestures, sweeping ones, two handed and symmetrical.

However, as Jews and Italians are assimilated into American culture, their gestures change. Second- and third-generation Americans take on the mannerisms of the culture they live in, that of the United States—another proof that gestures are not instinctive but are linked to culture.

The French use hand movements sparingly, but precisely and elegantly. The Germans, when they use hand movements, use them to reinforce statements about beliefs.

Women and men in business must be aware of these culturally linked gestures and their subtexts. It is difficult and sometimes awkward to try to change your gestures, but videotapes are useful in deciding whether to eliminate or tone down some of them. Other gestures may be eloquent and effective, and you may want to expand them.

WHAT SHOULD I DO WITH MY HANDS?

Gestures are made with the hands, and in any situation—a talk to business associates, a one-to-one encounter, or a boardroom discussion—you must be careful about which ones you use. I once saw a junior executive prepare a brilliant presentation for the board and then blow it all by delivering it with his hands in his pockets. Even worse than this are people who habitually jingle change or keys in their pockets as they talk. This is a gesture that can be interpreted as sexually provocative when men do it.

Speakers can also spoil their presentations by thrusting both hands into their jacket pockets while talking or by holding both hands clasped in front of them, a gesture whose subtext is an appeal—hardly fitting for someone making a forceful presentation.

The reason for these practices is the old stage problem that amateur actors face: What should I do with my hands? When you are speaking to a group, your hands can seem enormous and clumsy. It's a sign of an accomplished speaker when the hand movements are natural. In a talented speaker, they are not only natural but eloquent as well, adding to the delivery.

How can you learn to use your hands as an asset? There are two acceptable methods. One is practicing in front of a full-length mirror. Watch what you are doing and become aware of your gestures, of what they say and what they do not say. Understand the subtext of their movement.

The problem with this method is that you only see yourself

with biased eyes—your own—and you may not pick up little de-
fects. A better method is to enlist an audience of your friends
and colleagues to evaluate your performance. The best way to
handle this is to make a videotape of yourself in a mock presentation
or speech and play it back for your friends. Let them point out
your weaknesses, then play it over and over until you yourself
see these weaknesses and understand them. A second tape could
be made to eliminate the trouble spots. For some, two tapes will
do it. For others, half a dozen or more may be needed.

In a recent seminar on gesture and subtext, I taped an executive
in a mock presentation to his board of directors. He was a man
who had been in business for many years, yet watching himself
was a startling and revealing experience. "My God!" He shook
his head in shock. "I wring my hands when I talk. I never realized
I do that. What an asinine thing to do!" It took him only one
tape to change.

While it's important to learn the proper hand gestures, it's equally
important to make sure that the gestures are natural and not artificial
or used to excess. Excessive or random gestures diminish the
strength of your delivery. Gestures must accentuate and confirm
your words, not distract from or contradict them. Watch the gestures
of the person you are talking to or the audience you are addressing
and try to understand what their hands are telling you.

THE RITUALS OF NERVOUSNESS

It is not only the hands that can send out different subtexts but
also what the hands hold. Tapping a pencil or fiddling with a
bracelet or earring can send a subtext of nervousness, uncertainty,
uneasiness, or tension.

Stroking the arm of a chair, fingering a glass or a pen or even absently stroking part of your body, an arm or a leg, sends a subtext of loneliness, a need for comfort.

But a controlled use of objects can be of value. It can discharge nervous energy in a positive fashion. The key to this is that the object used must be an appropriate one. A pen or pencil with a pad of paper is particularly appropriate in a boardroom. The use of objects like these signals that you are making notes and are abreast of things.

These objects can be involved in elaborate rituals to help absorb nervousness. Aligning the pad and pencil, tapping the pencil once or twice against the teeth (thoughtfulness), removing your eyeglasses and replacing them, even using them to point—all these little rituals have their use. But it is best to rehearse and limit these movements so that they do not become nervous mannerisms themselves.

One woman executive makes a routine of removing her glasses when someone makes a statement she disagrees with, tapping her teeth with the temple, frowning, and replacing her glasses. The subtext: "I don't really believe what you've said."

Another CEO will stand up after hearing a statement he doesn't like, pause dramatically while taking up his pencil and pad, make a note, then turn to face the person with whom he disagrees. This sends an intimidating and unnerving subtext.

SYMBOLIC GESTURES

Symbolic gestures can also carry subtexts. In Europe, during the recent great changes in the communist countries, a constant gesture repeated by thousands in crowds was the V for victory sign. The subtext of that gesture was a damning indictment of the way the leaders had governed.

In the United States, the middle finger pointed upward is a sign of great insult. News stories keep surfacing of men shooting at someone who has given them the "finger." Jackie Mason, the comic, was blacklisted by the Ed Sullivan show many years ago for allegedly making this gesture which Sullivan thought was directed at him.

Symbolic gestures, ones you make deliberately because they represent a known subtext, are extremely important. A study involving twenty-five different countries and twelve thousand people examined twenty symbolic gestures. They found that few gestures could be limited to one country only, although Italy seemed to have the greatest number of symbolic gestures.

Many of these have come to the United States and are used here, particularly in Italian-American environments. Eight of the most significant ones are listed on the facing page.

The importance of knowing and understanding these gestures is apparent when you realize that in Europe, even today, certain gestures can bring police prosecution. In Germany, drivers making "the temple screw" at other drivers have been arrested and prosecuted! In England, the V for victory sign, if made with the palm facing out, is a dire insult.

These symbolic gestures are very much linked to particular cultures. For example, in Argentina, suicide is symbolized by an extended forefinger to the temple, mimicking a gun. In Japan it is an imaginary hara-kiri, a sword slice up the belly.

In a foreign country, you can run into trouble if you use the wrong hand sign. Dr. Robert Saitz and Edward Cervenka, in their

GESTURE	HOW IT IS DONE	THE SUBTEXT
Kissing the Fingertips	Pursing the fingers of the right hand. Raising them to the lips and kissing them as the hand is flicked away.	Praise or salutation
The Hand Purse	The fingers and thumb of one hand are straightened, brought together and pointed upward, palm toward the body.	A query
The Cheek Screw	Putting the forefinger into the center of the cheek and rotating it.	Good
The Temple Screw	Pressing the forefinger against the temple and rotating it.	Crazy
The Eyelid Pull	The forefinger pulls down the lower lid of the eye	I see what's going on, or watch out
The Ring	Thumb and forefinger make a circle as the hand is held up, palm out.	Okay
The Ear Tug	The earlobe is tugged by the fingers of one hand	A warning, or you are effeminate
The Nose Tap	The forefinger is placed alongside the nose	Be alert

Handbook of Gestures, cite an example that occurred in Colombia. There, the hand held out, palm down, is used to indicate the height of animals, never of humans. A lecturer from the States used this gesture to indicate the size of preschool children. This inadvertent misuse of a symbolic gesture broke up the class and made him an object of laughter. This is why anyone dealing with a foreign culture, at home or abroad, should know not only the culture's language but also its symbolic gestures and their subtexts.

5

BODY LANGUAGE: GESTURES, POSTURE, AND SPACE

THE POSTURE OF YOUTH

Gestures alone send a subtext, but they are far from the only signals a person sends out. Only movement combined with gestures gets to the whole truth. The entire body shapes the subtext even as our vocal cords shape our words. An executive entering a board-room sends an immediate message to the people gathered there.

Posture determines the subtext; the way he or she walks, sits, or moves gives the other clues.

An upright body sends a subtext of competence, pride, and assurance. Slumped over, the shoulders slack, the subtext is vulnerability, which, in most people's minds, is linked to uncertainty and uneasiness.

In one of my jobs, I worked with a senior executive who was in her seventies, successfully resisting retirement. When I went with her to a business meeting, I had to remind myself that she was not a young woman.

There were two subtextual reasons for the youthful impression she gave. She wore clothes that helped conceal her age—a long-sleeved dress with a high neck—and she fought against gray hair with a clever coloring job. She dressed in the best of taste, stylish and chic.

The real deception, however, lay in her posture. She moved like a young woman. She rose and sat effortlessly with none of the groaning or creaking of age. She sat erect and transmitted a regal quality with her back and shoulders—and, best of all, her voice was easy and youthful.

It was a triumph of body language, image projection, and posture over age. There is a lesson here for aging executives who want to send out a subtext of youth and vigor. Dyeing the hair to keep its natural color and plastic surgery to disguise jowls and wattles all help, but in both men and women the key to appearing youthful is posture and voice. Speaking firmly without hesitation sends a forceful message. Moving easily, not cautiously, standing and sitting upright, and getting up and sitting down with ease all contribute to a younger subtext, a subtext of vigor and strength.

READING PEOPLE'S POSTURE

Women send revealing subtexts about themselves not only by the way they sit, stand, and walk, but also by the way they carry their breasts. With shoulders forward and breasts pulled in and minimized, the subtext is "I am ashamed of my body." It is impossible to signal confidence and certainty with this posture.

With men, the abdomen and belly are the vulnerable areas. When a man tightens his belly and lets his abdominal muscles pull his stomach taut, the message sent is "I am aware of you. I want to make an impact on you." The subtext: strength.

The person who leans back in his chair as he listens to someone else is pulling away from involvement. Leaning forward signals intensity and interest.

All these statements are generally true, but they are generalizations. Not everyone uses the same posture to send the same subtext. There are cultural and regional differences in posture. In her book *Male and Female*, anthropologist Margaret Mead noted that all men do not cross their legs in the same way, nor do they move and sit in similar postures. The behavior of each American, she noted, is an imperfectly realized version of the behavior of others. The postures of Americans are the result of the melting pot of our culture.

People who like each other or agree with each other tend to mirror each other's posture. In a business meeting, when people share a point of view, they tend to share a posture. When one person in a group changes position, the other group members will usually shift position to match. If one member of the group disagrees with the others, his or her posture will disagree as well.

In a discussion in any group or gathering, whether it's a boardroom meeting or a negotiating session, the leader will often adopt a posture that the others, as they agree, will copy. Anyone holding out will invariably adopt a different posture until he or she is convinced.

One CEO told me that in a negotiating session he will often mimic the posture of the leader of the opposition and in a sense "feel out" the other's subtext. "It gives me some insight into their problems. I find that I get a better idea of whatever my opponent feels. It also helps create rapport. In a way, they feel I'm on their side."

Here are some clues to reading the subtexts of others by their posture:

- A modified military posture can signify formality.
- Facing someone directly with the eyes, face, shoulders, and upper body sends a subtext of rapt attention.
- Turning the body away as one talks, facing sideways and avoiding eye contact, sends a subtext of reluctance, of "I don't want to be involved." It's a subtle snub.
- Walking erect sends a subtext of certainty—"I'm in charge here."

The strong subtext behind posture was made clear in the famous trial of the Chicago Seven in the 1960s. Defense attorney William Kunstler objected to Judge Julius Hoffman's posture. During the prosecutor's summation, the judge leaned forward, which sent out a subtext of attention and interest. When the defense made its summation, he leaned back in his chair, in such a relaxed manner that he seemed half-asleep.

Kunstler pointed out that these postures and their subtexts clearly were attempts to influence the jury. The objection was overruled, but it nevertheless made the jury and the press covering the trial aware of what Kunstler felt was the judge's prejudiced attitude.

Social subtexts are often reflected quite simply in posture. If, in talking to someone, you lean forward, the unspoken subtext is "I like you." If you lean back while sitting, or turn slightly away while standing, the subtext is "I don't like you." Are you threatened by the other person? You will tend to sit up straight, almost as if you were on the defensive, ready to jump into action.

There are differences in the social subtexts sent by the sexes. A man will sit up, on the alert, if he feels threatened by another man, but he will not do this with a woman. Instead, he is likely to lounge back. However, it is rare for a woman to sit at attention if she feels threatened. She is more likely to move away from the threat, to move back. As more and more women are integrated into the world of business, however, these signals tend to change. Women are beginning to use the same signals as men in jockeying for power and position.

ATTENTION, AGGRESSION, AND DEFENSE

Traditionally, someone who sits with arms and legs in an open posture sends a subtext of being receptive to new ideas and suggestions. Closed arms and legs indicate disagreement (though a woman wearing a skirt will of course choose to close her legs regardless of her attitude). How the head is held, a smile or the lack of a smile, the slant of the shoulders, all amplify the subtext.

Watch the posture of people at office gatherings or meetings. Those outside the action hold different postures from those involved with what is going on. Outsiders stand with their weight on one foot rather than both. Someone more closely involved stands with the weight on both feet leaning forward and with head held forward. Leaning away from a situation signals disinterest, noninvolvement, distaste.

As with the subtexts for liking and disliking, the subtext for paying attention depends on posture. The degree to which you face the person you are talking to indicates the amount of attention you are paying to that person. Face someone squarely with your upper body, increase eye contact, and lean toward that person and the subtext is "I am paying attention to you."

Stand with the body turned away and only occasionally turn your head to face the other, and the message is "I am paying only a minimal amount of attention." Turn away altogether and you terminate the conversation. There is an insulting subtext in this posture if it is done while the other person is talking.

If more than two people, standing or sitting one on either side, are talking to you, it's difficult to pay attention to both. This dilemma is usually solved by turning one part of the body to one person and the rest to the other. You might incline your head to the one on the right while the rest of your body faces left. From time to time, alternate positions. The subtext is obviously "I am interested in what both of you are saying."

Then status comes into play. The higher the status of the person you are talking to, the more inclined you are to face him or her. While the face-to-face confrontation sends a subtext of attention, it is also a necessary posture for dominance. Facing that person, standing and moving toward him or her, combined with an aggressive stare, sends a clear subtext of dominance.

An executive can assume a loose and relaxed position during discussions, but when a forceful statement is needed, a shift to an aggressive posture emphasizes the statement.

How do you send a subtext of aggression? With a grim face, clenched fists, a slight crouch if standing, the body angled forward, eye contact held as long as possible.

A defensive tension shows itself in tightly folded arms, a straight back, head half turned away, and the avoidance of eye contact.

THE MESSAGE IN THE WALK

Posture, of course, includes walking. The stride and pace of an executive as he or she enters a boardroom can radiate a dozen different subtexts ranging from confidence to ineptitude. Generally, people who walk rapidly and swing their arms freely send a subtext of being goal oriented. People who scuff along, head down, signal dejection. Those who walk with their hands on their hips, a male posture adopted by Winston Churchill in the Second World War, send a subtext of "I want to get where I'm going in the shortest possible time."

The preoccupied walk, slow paced, head lowered, hands clasped behind, is private, thoughtful: "I'm considering all sides of the question." The "Benito Mussolini" walk, a man's walk, consists of chin raised arrogantly, arms swinging, legs stiff in a sort of strut: "I am an important person!"

The "model's" walk, a woman's walk, is almost a glide. The body sways, but remains erect. The subtext is sultry and provocative and totally unsuited for business!

In 1985, an article in *The New York Times* described Ronald Reagan's posture during a discussion with a reporter. Reagan has been generally held to be a master at using posture to get a subtext across. The article reads like a summary of many of the points I've made on posture:

"For much of the time Mr. Reagan settled back comfortably . . . as he warmed to the give and take, his responses came punctuated with a little shake of the head, a smile, a sign of emphasis here and there or a hand reached out to gesture." When the issue of Star Wars came up, "his body language changed. He became totally engaged. He leaned his body into the discussion, moving forward in his chair." When the talk turned to Soviet violations, "he put . . . his back straight against the chair." Take some lessons from a master!

SPACE: THE FINAL FRONTIER

We rarely think of space when we think of body language and the subtext it conveys, but manipulation of space can be an important business tool. Take the case of Mark, a canny CEO trying to engineer a takeover of a rival company.

The other company was headed by Harper, who thought he knew a lot about the subtext of power. He decided to show Mark who was the boss from the very beginning. To demonstrate his independence and importance, Harper told his staff to arrive at the meeting fifteen minutes after it was scheduled to start.

"Time is a powerful weapon," he told his assistant. "Being fifteen minutes late will keep them guessing. It'll make Mark anxious, and I'll be able to exploit that anxiety and throw him off target from the very start."

It was a clever ploy, but Mark was sharper. He arrived at the meeting room a few minutes early, surveyed the situation, and took in the battlefield—a long, oval conference table. Like any good commander, Mark took advantage of the absence of his enemy to place himself in the most strategic seat at the end of the table facing the door. He knew that this would remain the dominant position only if he could prevent Harper from taking the seat at the other end of the table. So he placed Jane, his executive VP, at the other end of the table and flanked her with two of his staff. He then placed two more of his associates on either side of his chair.

By time Harper arrived, his late ploy, often effective, had backfired because of Mark's territorial triumph. Mark earned another victory when he stood up and held his hand out as Harper entered, forcing his rival to walk all the way around the table in order to shake his hand.

Confused by the turn of events, Harper was flustered and quickly took one of the only seats open to him, a subordinate one. Had he been a wiser man, he would have simply asked Jane to move and then sat in her power place, making it a more equal battle. By not doing this, he lost control of the situation. Mark became the one projecting the subtext of power and took full advantage of it in dealing with his adversary.

In this case, the subtext of power and status came from a clever use of the space around the conference table. The legendary King Arthur was well aware of this technique, when Merlin advised him to use a round table for his knights. In that way no one would have higher status than anyone else.

Unfortunately, this doesn't work when one person, such as a king, has a great deal of status from the start. No matter what the shape of the table, the people seated next to the king have the highest status, and status declines as one is seated farther from the king.

In a boardroom or conference room the person with the highest status will usually choose one end of an oblong or oval table. The exception is the person of very high status, the CEO or chairman of the board who is aware of the cachet such a position gives and wants to appear approachable. In that case, he or she will often take a center position at the side of the table. However, this democratic move is usually defeated by the others who range themselves alongside the leader in decreasing order of importance, much as the knights did around King Arthur.

OFFICE SPACE

A knowledge of the byplay of seating arrangements is important in office politics. How does the boss sit in relation to a client? Should you use a desk or a couch or two chairs at a coffee table?

A desk can serve as a protective device to keep the client at a distance and assert just who is in charge here. This is the boss's territory, and the client is here on sufferance. It's best to use this "protective" desk to sit behind if you want to send a subtext of formality with no levity, no equality.

If you wish to reduce the formality, the client's chair should be placed at the side of the desk, with only the corner between the two of you. This is a more comfortable arrangement, and it cuts the interacting space down to an intimate distance.

You can be even more informal by getting away from the desk altogether. For just this reason, many business offices have a couch, a low coffee table, and visitors' chairs. Discussing business in this setting sends a subtext of equality.

If both people choose the couch to sit on, the positioning of their bodies, whether they incline toward each other or away, sends clues about their relationship. One arm along the back of the couch, the body inclined toward the other, sends a subtext of involvement and interest. Inclining the body away from the other, using the arm between almost as a guard, indicates disbelief, a desire to resist.

The use of space to send subtexts works on many levels outside of the office. At a business lunch, there is usually an unspoken division of territory when two people sit down on opposite sides of a small table. An invisible line drawn midway between the two splits the table into two fields, one for each diner. If one diner begins to move his or her plate, utensils, and glass into the other's space, it becomes an aggressive act. The aggression may not be perceived consciously, but there is a psychological reaction, an invasion of privacy. People react to this perceived invasion in various ways, depending on how friendly they are and how introverted or extroverted the reacting person is.

However, when both diners see the space between them as appropriate, communication improves in depth and clarity. This is based upon the need of all people for space that is particularly theirs. At home we think: "It's my kitchen." "It's my den." "It's my room."

The need for private territory extends to all walks of life. In business we are often judged by the size and condition of our office. The larger the office, the stronger the subtext of importance. A window increases the importance. A corner office with two windows is most desirable. Office furniture sends a message of worth. A desk and two chairs are at the bottom of the scale. A desk, chairs, couch, coffee table, and a bar are at the top.

MANIPULATING SPACE

We carry this same need for space around with us. When we talk to someone, we, in the States, prefer a distance of two feet between talkers. We feel comfortable at that distance. In other countries people want to be close enough to "feel the other's breath." When we walk into a theater without reserved seats we try to manage a seat with no one on either side. The same is true in a bus or subway. Unless all the seats are filled, we resist sitting next to someone, and we resent someone sitting next to us.

This is how we react to space on a two-dimensional level, but we also react to it in three dimensions. Height gives dominance. Height sends a slight subtext of intimidation. A friend of mine, a salesman, is six feet four inches tall. "When I talk to a potential customer," he told me, "I always manage to minimize my height. I either sit on the edge of a desk if we are both standing, or I try to seat myself so that I'll be lower. Sometimes I have to slump a bit to do it. The point is, I don't want the customer to think I'm pressuring him, dominating him."

Of course, there are times when my friend takes advantage of his height in order to loom over someone when intimidation is a useful tool! This use of height is similar to an invasion of space. Some people deliberately use spatial invasion to send a particular subtext. A manual on criminal interrogation and confession, for instance, directs interrogating officers to sit close to the subject without a table or desk between them, since the table or desk can give the subject a sense of safety and relief. It is a protection of sorts, and doing away with it leaves the subject more vulnerable.

The police officer is also directed, once interrogation begins, to move the chair in closer, doing it subtly until one of the officer's knees is between the subject's. This intense spatial invasion can be so upsetting that the subject will often break down and tell the police just what they want to know.

I have seen job interviewers use a less intense variation of this same technique; moving in to violate the applicant's space often knocks down the artificial defenses put up to persuade the interviewer. It is not a very kind technique!

In considering how each of us uses space, we should be aware that the way people react to invasions of their personal space depends on their perception of that space. Some people have pathologically distorted ideas about their own zones of privacy. Dr. Augustus F. Kinzel, a social scientist, studied prisoners and concluded that some are violence prone because their normal zone of privacy, which should be about four feet, had expanded to six feet or more. When someone got what they perceived as "too close," they reacted with panic and then violence.

There are times when even "normal" people seem to have needs for extended space; driving an automobile is such a time. You can make a driver extremely nervous by tailgating. It is as if the zone of privacy surrounding the driver extends to surround the automobile as well, reaching out a couple of car lengths in front and back. When someone is cut off by a car moving into his or her zone, there is a sudden spurt of anger. Many drivers react by racing to cut the other driver off in turn. It's like the violent prisoner's reaction to what he perceives as crowding.

Another variation in personal spatial needs is linked to personality. A psychiatrist, Dr. William E. Peipold, tested people to discover if they had introverted or extroverted personalities. He then measured the distance they placed themselves from an interviewer.

He concluded that introverts sat farther away from people than extroverts. People who were praised moved closer and people under stress moved away. The more comfortable a person is with another, the closer the distance between them.

A subtle job interviewer can read a number of different subtexts from the movements of the applicants during an interview.

6

INSIDE OUT

The subtext sent out by your inner feelings is often a key element in the way you relate to other people. Different personality traits send out very distinct subtextual messages. Three internal characteristics in particular that make an impact on others are risk taking, flexibility, and empathy.

SUBTEXT OF RISK

The subtext that you send out when you take a risk, when you chance something, is one of confidence and aggressiveness. The very act of going out on a limb says to people that you are a person of action.

A group of us were sitting on the deck of my friend Steve's house one evening watching the sun set over the Pacific. Steve, who had been tossing pennies into the bubbling hot tub claiming it acted as a wishing well, said, "I saw a job I could apply for the other day. Selling fax machines. It said absolutely no experience needed. They have their own list of customers."

I smiled. Steve was a compulsively successful Hollywood writer who had once confessed to me that he had more money than he knew what to do with. "So you're job hunting," I said.

"Well, I read the want ads. There was one for a retired couple to look after an estate out in the valley, but my wife says I'm not retired yet." He tossed another coin into the hot tub. "You know, I never had a real job. I started writing and selling right after the Korean war, and I was making a hundred a week before I was twenty. Whenever we got together, my dad used to ask me when I was going to get a real job. He'd come up with some position he'd heard about that paid forty or fifty dollars a week, but as he pointed out, it was real work." He hesitated, then in a serious voice added, "I guess what I want to find out is whether I could really hold down a job. It would be a risk to try it."

We were silent for a while, then Larry, an executive in a large industrial corporation, cleared his throat. "I think the risk is in changing jobs. I used to be a hospital administrator, and while I was good at it, I felt limited. I thought I was in a dead end. But, you know, I had no experience outside of hospital administration. My first job was doing their PR work, and I worked my way up the hospital hierarchy. The trouble was, I wanted something else, a position with more responsibility and more power, and I knew I couldn't get it there."

"What did you do?" someone asked.

"I picked the biggest corporation in my area, walked into the president's office, and asked for a job as his assistant. I knew I was taking a risk, but I also knew that if it paid off it would be worth it."

"What happened?"

"He talked to me for a while, then, with a rather cold look, said, 'You know, this job requires a tremendous amount of experience in corporate management plus an MBA.'

"Well, I think I was pretty cool myself when I answered, 'I haven't got an MBA.' But you know, an hour later I had that job!"

We were all silent for a moment, then Steve said, "I appreciate the drama of the situation, but why did he hire you?"

"Self-confidence," Larry answered. "Aggressive self-confidence. I told him I could do the job, and do it better than any other applicant, and I convinced him because I had convinced myself. It was a management job, and I was a great manager. My record at the hospital showed that. I was willing to take a risk because we both agreed that if I didn't work out in one month I'd be out, but I really felt it was worth the risk." He was silent for a moment, then he looked at Steve. "Do you honestly feel the risk of trying to work at a job at your age, of testing yourself, is really worth it?"

NOTHING VENTURED, NOTHING GAINED

Steve never took that particular risk. It was just a fantasy with him. There was no economic force driving him, nor was there the same thing that pushed Larry—the spirit of adventure, the need for wider opportunities, a chance at power.

But some weeks ago I read in *Variety* that Steve had indeed taken a risk, a long shot, motivated by the same spirit of adventure that moved Larry. Instead of selling his latest screenplay, he had decided to produce and direct the film himself. The point of it all, according to the article, was that now Steve would have complete control over his story. He had the power, and along with it the responsibility of the production—and the risk of failure.

All of us, no matter what level we operate on, must learn that we cannot gain power in a business unless we are willing to chance something, and to be responsible for our own risks.

Before you take a risk, you must know what the consequences are. Before Larry gave up his job as hospital administrator, he had to know just what would happen if he failed. Not all risks succeed. Although Larry did well, in a sink-or-swim situation he could have sunk. He could have found himself with a job he couldn't manage, and, after a month, without either job. He knew the risk, but still, he had this to say:

"You just can't go around taking risks like I did. You have to be responsible for your actions."

"But how did you manage it?"

"I think the head of the corporation sensed something in me, that told him I was aggressive enough to succeed. I think it was my willingness to take a risk. I knew exactly what I was doing and what the odds were. It worked for me."

Larry was aggressive enough to take that risk, and in taking it, he let his new boss see his subtext of determination.

YOUR INNER RISK FACTOR

For some of us, risk taking simply means adding up all the advantages and disadvantages, and then making the choice between them. But many of us cannot make that choice. We are just not strong enough to take the risk. Do you want to project that confident image of a risk taker? How do you determine your own inner risk factor?

You can do it through an evaluation of your own life and the number of times you gambled on important issues. Another help in determining it is a simple test. I have prepared ten questions, each with three possible answers. The only thing required is that you answer each question with absolute honesty.

Put aside all concerns about right and wrong, all questions of morality. You may feel that one answer is the right one, but the point is, be honest about what you would do, not what you think is *right* to do. No one is judging your answers except yourself. Think about your answers. Do they project a successful subtext?

One-Armed Bandits

You attend a convention in Nevada, and you must pass a bank of slot machines each day on your way to the meeting hall.

(A) You put all your quarters in each time you go past.

(B) You set aside an allotted amount to play with and stick to that amount.

(C) You ignore the machines. You're here for the convention.

Daring New Clothes

You're a man, and you like the way a bright orange tie looks with your suit, or, if you are a woman, you have just bought a rather extravagant blouse.

(A) You decide to wear it to work.

(B) You won't wear it to work, but you will wear it socially.

(C) You return it the next day and wonder what silly impulse made you buy it in the first place.

The Nasty Supervisor

You're working on a job, and your new supervisor is obnoxious.

(A) You tell him off.

(B) You treat him coolly.

(C) You pretend there's nothing wrong.

The Pickup

On a business trip, you meet a stranger on a plane and he/she is attractive, but you know nothing about him/her. She/he suggests that you meet for dinner that night.

(A) Sure. It might be fun.

(B) You suggest a foursome with another couple you know.

(C) Regretfully, you decline.

Relocating

The company you work for is relocating to a new area you know nothing about. They offer you better pay to relocate.

(A) You take it. It could be a good place to live, and the salary is worth it.

(B) You spend every minute down to the wire trying to guess what is right, to go or stay. Eventually you go because who knows if another job is available here?

(C) You decide not to go because you're too attached to the house and town you live in.

The Unknown Candidate

You're with a group of business associates discussing politics, and they mention a candidate whose name is unfamiliar.

(A) You ask who the candidate is.

(B) You join in carefully, hoping your ignorance won't be detected.

(C) You keep your mouth shut until the subject changes.

The Fabulous Vacation

Your vacation is coming up and a fellow worker tells you of a fabulous place she's gone to and urges you, if you want to go, to make a reservation at once. They're almost full up.

(A) You take her advice and make the reservation.

(B) Before you decide, you ask for more details and the names of other people who liked it.

(C) You settle for a place you know.

The Wrong Order

Your boss gives you an order you know is wrong.

(A) You question the order and tell him why.

(B) You do as he tells you, but feel uneasy all day. What if things go wrong and he blames you?

(C) You follow orders, but look for some way of covering up repercussions.

The Job Offer

You are doing a good job in your present position, but although the pay is right, you don't seem to be getting ahead. Another job offer comes up at the same salary, but with better chances of advancement.

(A) You take it at once. You really have nothing to lose.

(B) You do as much investigating of the other company as possible including talking to some of the people working there before you make a decision.

(C) You hang on to the job you have. At least you know the ropes here, and the situation can always change.

The Takeover

You run a small company with a very good potential. A multinational company makes a takeover offer that will leave you well provided for.

(A) You fight the offer. There's no telling how well your own company can do if you play your cards right.

(B) You resist for a while, but in the end the security of the settlement offered by the other company wins out and you capitulate.

(C) You agree to the takeover. After all, it will leave you secure for life.

SCORING

You should give yourself ten points for every (A) answer, eight for all the (B)'s and six for the (C)'s. If you get a score of 80 to

100, you are considered quite a gambler. Between 70 and 80 indicates someone who will take a sensible amount of risk, and a score of 60 to 70 indicates that you are not much of a risk taker.

The point to remember is that taking a risk is closely allied to your own potential for aggression, and thereby the subtext of aggressiveness that you send out to other people.

LEARNING TO RISK

What happens if you've tested yourself and you score a slim 60? You're obviously a person who doesn't gamble and who sends out an indecisive subtext. How do you change all that?

There are many reasons people fear risking, and the most common one is the fear of failure or of the humiliation of being rebuffed. People who honestly score 100 on the risking test have none of these fears. Perhaps they are unrealistic. One successful businessperson, the head of a large advertising firm, came up with a score over 90.

"I've usually gone for the long shots," he told me. "If I fail, so what? Am I any worse off than before? Failure is a part of the game. If you're afraid to fail, then you're afraid to try, and you're lost. You must understand that most failures don't mean that much. You can pick yourself up, dust yourself off, and start over again.

"The worst thing about being afraid to risk is that you give off an odor of fear, of uncertainty. Other people sense the person who can't take a risk. As for taking a chance, for every success I've had, I've also had half a dozen flops, but in the long run I've gotten ahead."

"All well and good," the timid starter says. "He can afford to talk big. He scored over 90. But I just can't summon up the courage to take the kind of chance that might change my life. What can I do?"

What we can all do if we're afraid of risking is to start small. Most people learn the art of risking as children. If they succeed in their first risks, they go on to bigger and better ones. If they don't succeed, if they're knocked down again and again, they grow fearful of trying and end up as timid starters.

EASY RISKS

If you are a timid starter, you have to make up for all those early failures. You can do it by starting with an easy risk, a meaningless risk. Use the telephone to avoid any face-to-face confrontation and the possibility of being overawed by someone else's manipulative subtext.

Try bucking the bureaucracy. For example, call the phone company about a mischarged call, or the utility company, or even a credit card outfit. Let yourself get angry, and if you wish, hang up on them. You'll feel a little tickle of power.

What have you accomplished? Well, for one thing you've gotten your feelings out. You've expressed a subtext of hostility or anger and you've survived. That's something!

FACE-TO-FACE RISKS

Now you're prepared for a face-to-face confrontation. Try it with a stranger in a situation that isn't important. Risk an argument with a shopkeeper or a waiter in a restaurant. Demand a better table, or send back a dish that isn't done properly. This takes a surprising amount of courage. Argue with a supermarket clerk about the price of an item, or get into a cab and tell the driver the exact route to take to get you where you're going—your way, not his or hers.

You may win out in some of these arguments, though sometimes it seems that it's a rare person who can win over a cab driver or a waiter. But the point of these trials is not to win, rather to experience the risk, to experience failure as well as success, to learn that risking and losing are not the end of the world. Taking risks will also strengthen the subtext that you send out.

The following risks are divided into classes A, B, and C, with C the easiest.

CLASS-C RISKS

Once you're comfortable with these warm-up exercises in asserting your own will, once your subtext is perceived in a positive way, you're ready to move on to some serious risking. In effect, you've tested your wings and found that you can fly.

Just as victory may have been less satisfactory than you thought it would be, failure may not be as devastating as you expected either. If you've survived the warm-up, then you're ready for some Class-C risks.

(1) Tell somebody off, whether it's a coworker, your lover or mate, your neighbor, sister or brother, parent, or even your child. The person you tell off shouldn't be someone above you, but an equal.

(2) Insist that your husband, wife, or lover do something you

want, something he or she is not eager to do—perhaps buying something or going somewhere, seeing a certain movie or television program. The point is, it must be something you want.

(3) Ask your boss or supervisor for the day off for personal matters. Don't give an excuse. Say you simply want the day off.

(4) If you are single, accept a blind date.

In all these, failure is as important as success because part of taking risks is understanding that the world doesn't end, the sky doesn't fall in, you can still show your face when someone says no. On the other hand, you can experience that little surge of accomplishment when it all works out.

CLASS-B RISKS

If you've survived the Class-C risks, you're ready to try your luck with the Class-B series. Again, don't move from one series to the next until you're comfortable with the previous one.

(1) If you are single, go to a singles' bar and talk to at least five strangers. If singles' bars turn you off, try talking to strangers at a museum or a movie.

(2) Ask your boss for a raise.

(3) Ask your supervisor for more responsibility and explain why you can handle it.

(4) Take a part of your savings and invest it.

CLASS-A RISKS

If you've managed to get through Class-B risking intact, see if you can think up five other risks on the same level, and try them out. If you can do this in a comfortable way, then you are ready for Class A. These are higher risks and should not be taken lightly. You must be sure you want them and are ready for their dangers as well as their rewards.

Of course, no one takes all of them, but at least one is necessary to demonstrate the two fundamental rules about risking. You cannot get ahead in life without taking risks, and you *can* survive the failure of any risk.

(1) Change your job if you don't like what you are doing. This risk is linked to age. In your twenties it is almost a Class-B risk. In your thirties it is more serious, and in your forties it is a full-fledged Class A. There are people who have changed jobs successfully in their fifties and sixties, but it is a much harder step and the risk is far greater then.

(2) Buy a house or an apartment. Many people feel this risk is so great that they defer it all their lives. If you have sound reasons for not buying your home, try moving, changing to a better neighborhood. (Note: There must be sound reasons and some advantage involved. Take a risk because in some way it will help your condition, not just for risk's sake.)

(3) If you have never worked, go out and get a job.

(4) If you've always wanted to be your own boss, give up your job and go into business for yourself. On a business level this is one of the greatest risks of all and one you should never take without knowing all the consequences, as well as advantages.

(5) Just as starting your own business is the greatest risk on a business level, getting married may be the greatest risk on a personal level—although many people argue that staying single is a greater risk. If you have been contemplating marriage, go ahead and take the plunge.

These are suggestions for Class-A risks. By now you should

understand just what such a risk is and you can devise your own in line with your life-style and needs.

AN ABILITY FOR FLEXIBILITY

Flexibility in a person projects an image of being accommodating. It indicates someone who is willing to make things work in a way that is not threatening to others. A flexible person's subtext says "I'll work *with* you."

One of the people I talked to in gathering material for this book was a self-made millionaire. He had built a small grocery store in Chicago into a huge, multinational chain of supermarkets. When I asked for one "key" to the secret of his success, he laughed. "It's not as simple as that. Maybe hard work, determination . . ." He shook his head. "No, actually, if I had to pin it down to one thing I'd say it was because I was never afraid to change horses in midstream."

At my blank look, he explained himself. "If I started something, a store in what I soon realized was a bad location, and I saw that it wasn't working out, I'd give it up right away and find some other location. And it wasn't only location. That's just an example. When *anything* didn't work out, I wouldn't hold on. I'd take a close, hard look to see if it was as good as I thought, and if it wasn't, I'd give up on it and try something else. You have to know when to persist, but you also have to know when to quit."

"Did that apply to people, too?" I asked.

He shrugged. "Maybe I was ruthless, but I think I was just realistic. If employees didn't work out, I dropped them. I never let myself be locked into anything, nor was I too rigid. You know, if I had to sum up my success in one word, I'd say flexibility."

Many of us have the wrong idea about flexibility. We think of it as a weakness, a form of vacillation, an inability to make a firm decision. We see a flexible person as someone willing to take second best, who sends out a subtext of uncertainty.

But we should look at flexibility from another point of view: If you are a flexible person, you don't limit yourself. You understand the importance of switching your goals if your original goal is impossible to reach, or if the difficulty in reaching it is not worth the end result. If one approach doesn't work out, the flexible person doesn't persist in it. You cut your losses and move to a more logical and workable solution.

Flexibility requires a particular kind of philosophy. The flexible person is continually reevaluating goals. You question yourself about the importance of those goals, and above all you are able to fight the clichés of our culture. Boiled down, it becomes a matter of testing reality at every step.

Will this approach cause us to give up the vaunted American Dream? We've been taught that if we set our sights on something and go after it, we will succeed. All it takes is hard work and determination, and someday we can be president, if not of the nation, then of General Motors.

Must you give up this dream if you adopt a flexible approach? Perhaps, but you must realize that it might only be a dream. Understand the odds against it. Set goals, but realize how realistic those goals are.

TESTING YOUR FLEXIBILITY

One important aspect of flexibility is the recognition of alternative solutions. If your job demands that you get from New York to

Washington, D.C., and the airport is snowed in, you try for a ticket on the Metroliner. If that isn't running, you try the bus station, or you rent a car. Before giving up on your ultimate goal, you search for every possible way of realizing that goal.

The first step toward any goal is understanding the reality of that goal. Can you reach it?

The second step is to test your motivation. How much do you want to get there? Enough to warrant the attempt?

If both answers are yes, then you take the third step and examine all the different routes to the goal.

Here are three problems that can help you to decide how flexible you are, or how rigid. Each concerns someone boxed into an apparent dead end—yet each problem can be solved by a flexible approach. Consider each, and list all the possible solutions that occur to you.

If you see no way out, be careful! You are much too rigid and so you are sending a rigid, uncooperative subtext to the world around you.

If you can find two or three solutions, you are extremely flexible and headed for better things not only in the workplace but in your private life as well.

If you can find only one solution, you are still able to cope. The faster you find a solution, the more flexible you are.

The Hotshot Salesman

Dan is executive vice president in charge of sales at International Data Systems. Lou is one of IDS's top salespeople, and he has just approached Dan for a sizable raise.

Dan feels Lou deserves a raise. His record has been terrific, but Dan has laid down some rigid rules linking raises to seniority.

He knows a company must be consistent, and Lou hasn't nearly enough seniority for the money he wants. But he also knows that Lou is top-notch, and any number of competing firms are ready to hire him away. What should he do?

The DINKS

Tim and Nancy are your quintessential DINKS (Double Income, No Kids). They both have good jobs located within short commuting distance of their new house, purchased recently with great delight after years of saving for a down payment.

Now Nancy has been offered a very good job in the field she has wanted to enter, but the job is located just too far away to make commuting viable. Should she take the job?

The Tough CEO

Tiffany has just been offered a promotion to executive assistant for the CEO of her division. The salary is much better, but Tiffany has managed very well on what she gets working for her present boss whom she likes tremendously.

The CEO is a tough man to work for and demands a great deal more overtime than Tiffany is willing to put in. However, turning down the promotion will be bad for her future at the company. What's the best choice for her?

A SUBTEXT OF CONFIDENCE

Each of these short scenarios seems like a dead end, but there are "outs" that depend on a flexible mode of thinking. The flexible person is a creative coper, one sensible enough to recognize a dead end and search for a workable alternative. The flexible person can shift gears and change approach when things aren't working out. Best of all, the flexible person sends out a subtext of confidence. He or she says, "I believe that I can make things work, even if I have to choose another way to do it."

The flexible person is the one people usually turn to when a problem arises. If you are like that, you are constantly aware of reality, and this awareness will teach you how much you can achieve in any deadlocked situation. You not only know when to stop trying, but also when to keep trying when there is a realistic chance of success.

A deeper recognition of flexibility as a way to project a positive subtextual image will allow you to use it to influence other people. Parents using a little flexibility can move children in almost any direction. Teachers can influence pupils, and supervisors can influence the people under them.

The key to it all is to abolish rigidity. At crucial intervals, reexamine your motives, goals, and procedures. Each time, recognize whether you are locked into the wrong path or committed to the right one.

EMPATHY AND THE METHOD

The third inner trait that sends out a positive image to others is the ability to participate in another's feelings: empathy. Empathy evokes a subtext of concern and interest in other people. It wins confidence!

"You don't understand what I've been through," the salesman tells his manager, almost frantically. "You don't know what it's like out there on the street!"

"I've got problems you can't begin to comprehend," the frustrated executive tells the union representative.

"You've got problems? You try a stint on the line, and you'll learn what problems really are!" the union rep shoots back.

"I can't do it," the receptionist tells the lawyer who has just brought out a pile of briefs for filing. "You don't understand the mess I have out here."

"You don't understand." "You don't know what it's like." "You can't begin to comprehend!" The obvious messages behind all these statements are frustration, anger, complaint. The not-so-obvious subtext is the speaker's perception of a lack of empathy in the person he or she is dealing with.

Simply stated, empathy is the ability to understand someone else's feelings and problems. Empathy is a means for projecting a very necessary subtext of understanding, sensitivity, and concern.

Is empathy something we either have or don't have? Can we learn it? If we have some degree of empathy, is there any way to increase it?

Some of us seem to be born with a natural sense of empathy. We constantly hear of children who empathize with a parent's grief, who understand each other's hurts and pains. Little Johnny will cry when his friend Max hurts his finger. Sara will burst into tears when Emma's doll is broken. In fact, many studies conclude that all children have a natural sense of empathy, which decreases by some degree as they grow up.

But even in those of us in whom empathy seems lost, a residue remains, and it is possible to develop that latent empathy and discover how to use it as a coping tool.

The "Method" school of acting gives us a clue to how this can be done. The Method is, essentially, based on the learning and development of empathy. To play a part, the actor must learn more than lines and how to deliver them. He or she is taught to understand the motivation behind the character. In a broader sense, the actor is taught to empathize, not with a real person, but with the character in the play or film. Is the character logical in what he or she is doing, in the speeches being delivered, in his or her action? What makes the character say and do these things?

When the Method works and empathy with the character takes over, the actor empathizes completely with the character for the duration of the play or film, often to the point where there is difficulty getting out of the part afterward. The Method is a rather difficult approach to acting, but, if done properly, it can be very effective and moving. Dustin Hoffman is an actor devoted to this method, and often he lives the life of the character he portrays before doing the role. His parts become tremendously convincing because his subtext sensed by the audience is that of the character, not of Hoffman.

Tim Pigott-Smith, the gifted actor who portrayed villainous policeman Ronald Merrick in the British television production of "The Jewel in the Crown," explained in a *New York Times* interview how he was able to empathize with Merrick:

"I sat in front of a mirror with my jaw thrust out so that the lips went down and forced themselves into a sneer. By the end I could switch this look on, and as an actor, if you can throw the physical switch, the mental process of the character will follow," and the correct subtext will be projected.

SELF-EMPATHY

Sometimes the ability to empathize with yourself, in terms of what you felt during some previous experience, will send a helpful subtext to your inner self. In a sense, you will be using the Method to convince yourself of something. A successful trial lawyer I talked to summed this up very succinctly:

"When I was in college, I was on the debating team. I remember one debate where I had a fantastic edge over my opponent. I knew all the facts. I knew how to present them in logical and impressive order, and halfway through the debate it became apparent that my opponent was not really as well prepared as I was. I was filled with a quiet sense of confidence. I knew I couldn't lose, and I didn't.

"Now, when I'm making my final plea to the jury, I remember that moment, recall it vividly, and I can dredge up that same air of confidence, of certainty in my conviction. It works. Believe me. The subtext of my delivery becomes very impressive and convincing!"

Lawyers often rely heavily on empathy. They want a jury to empathize with them and with their client. It is a well-known fact that, taking the same words from a transcript, two different lawyers can ask the same questions or deliver the same speech and yet send very different subtexts to the jury.

Another very successful lawyer told me, "My secret is empathy. Not only do I try to get the jury to empathize with me and my client, but I also empathize with them. I put myself in their place, and by doing that I understand how they will react to me. That's why I try to get as much information about the jury members as I can during the initial interviews. I want to see if they'll empathize with my client, sure, but it's also so I can empathize with them." In other words, she knows what subtext to send out.

I once had an opportunity to talk to Lily Tomlin after she had done a bit from her very popular routine portraying a mildly sadistic telephone operator. I asked her how she managed to send out such a perfect subtext of her character. "Even the twisting of your foot when you needle a customer is the perfect gesture of a satisfied sadist," I remarked. "The vague caressing of your breast sends a subtext of sadness and loneliness that adds to the depth of the character. How do you do it?"

Tomlin hesitated, frowning. Then, with a little smile, she shook her head. "I honestly don't know. I never realized that caressing myself signified loneliness until you mentioned it, but it does, of course. What I do," she said carefully, "is become the woman. I get into her, feel the way she feels, think the way she thinks, and then everything flows from that. I do what she would do, not what I, as an actress, think is right."

TRADING PLACES

Based on the ideas behind the Method, role reversal is one of the best techniques for learning to empathize with someone else. I had an experience with this some time ago when I worked for a small drug company based in New York.

After five years of flawless work, the secretary to the head of sales told her boss that she was quitting. I was in Tom's office when Linda dropped this bombshell, and Tom shook his head in bewilderment. "You can't do this to me!" He turned to me. "She's the best girl I ever had!" Then he said to Linda, "This place will go to pot without you. If it's a raise . . ."

Linda shook her head. "Money has nothing to do with it. It's . . . Well, it's your attitude."

"My attitude?" Tom was genuinely confused. "What have I done?" He looked at me. "Have I done anything wrong?"

Linda elaborated. "Like calling me the best girl you ever had: I'm not! I'm almost forty and I have three kids. I'm not a girl! You just don't see me. I'm not a person to you. I'm a piece of furniture until you want something, then you treat me as if I were fifteen years old!"

Turning to me, Tom said helplessly, "What am I going to do? I can't get along without her."

I looked at both of them. "I tell you what I think you should do. I think you should try a game of role reversal for a couple of days." When they both looked puzzled, I explained. "Not work. Tom, you sure couldn't do Linda's work even if she could do yours, but why don't you try reversing the way you treat each other?"

Grasping at straws, Tom agreed at once. Linda was dubious at first, but caught on quickly. As the days passed, she called her boss by his first name, praised him to her associates—"That boy is a good worker"—ordered him about as casually as he had ordered her, and accepted the coffee he brought her without bothering to thank him.

In turn, Tom went all out. He called her Mrs. Bloom, asked her if she'd please do this or that, and in general, treated her as an assistant treats a boss.

"It opened both our eyes," Linda told me a week later as we rode down in the elevator. "I'm staying on now, and I can see how a boss can sometimes forget about an assistant's humanity. As long as Tom remembers that I need respect, too, I think things will work out."

"I think the little game you suggested helped me become sensitive to Linda as a human being," Tom told me over lunch. "It wasn't easy for me because I was giving up my dominant role, but it made me realize how arrogant I had been!"

DOING WHAT COMES NATURALLY

Many people don't need to practice role reversal to feel empathy for someone and project a subtext of concern. Feeling empathy comes naturally to them, and it helps in their dealings with family, friends, and lovers, as well as on the job. The saleswoman with a strong sense of empathy understands her clients. She senses when the moment is right for a hard sell, or when to hold back or try a soft sell, because she feels so much of what the client feels. Often she knows what the client feels without realizing that she does. She's a natural.

The labor mediator who is most successful is the one who feels empathy for both sides. He can put himself in the workers' shoes or the boss's because he senses how both feel. He appreciates their gripes and knows their weaknesses and strengths.

The father who is empathetic to his son can overcome the generation gap. He realizes how important it is for the boy to look like the other kids, to wear the same hairstyles and clothes. He understands how much his son needs to resist him and do things on his own because he can feel the way his son feels.

The same is true for mothers and their children—and may occur more frequently since women tend to have more empathy than men. Perhaps it is part of mothering, or perhaps the culture has more acceptance for the woman who is sensitive and receptive. By contrast, men are taught to be cool, to stand on their own two feet, and not be too sympathetic. Toughness is equated with manliness.

BREAKING THE BARRIERS

Among the things empathy can do is tear down the barriers between ages, races, classes, and religions. Jack, who taught English in a rough, urban area, found that his own education, mannerisms, speech, and color were all barriers between him and his students.

"When I first began teaching," he said, "it was like a nightmare. I wasn't used to kids like these. Oh, I had been warned, but the reality was way beyond my expectations. I came from a caring, middle-class family, and the kids knew it and disliked me for it. Maybe *disliked* is too gentle a word. They didn't trust me, and every day I'd find myself talking to a sea of closed, cold faces and eyes that said, *prove yourself*!

"I knew I couldn't make it, and I just wanted to get through that term and transfer or quit. Then, in an afternoon, it all changed. The principal suspected one boy, Darryl, of marking the blackboard with graffiti, but he couldn't prove it. I came into class one day and caught Darryl red-handed spraying the board.

"I took the can away, and we were both standing there in front of the class while I searched for something devastating and nasty to say. I really felt hateful. Then the door opened, and the principal walked in.

"He took in the situation and said, 'I see we have a little problem.' At that moment, I don't know why, everything shifted focus for me. Suddenly I knew what Darryl felt, the defiance, not maliciousness, that had gone into his graffiti. I felt empathy.

"I acted instinctively. I put my arm around Darryl's shoulders and smiled at the principal. 'Darryl's helping me to clean the board. I sprayed it so the class could see how hard it is to get paint off. It's a good object lesson, don't you think?'

"The principal was suspicious, but there was nothing he could do. Later he bawled me out for encouraging vandalism with my 'demonstration,' but the amazing thing was what happened to me, to Darryl and the rest of the class. The barrier was down. We all understood each other, and I was on their side against unreasoning authority.

"The rest of the term was different—not great, but better. Darryl became my protector, and I was able to teach him and the rest of the class. There are still problems, and I guess there always will be, but now I empathize with the kids and they understand that I'm caring and concerned. I'm not transferring. I got through to them."

THE REVERSE LIST

The barriers this teacher faced were economic, cultural, and racial. Sometimes the barriers are religious or sexual. Such barriers often lead to a subtext that says "I don't understand you." Neither side knows what the other feels, and the subtext projected is one of suspicion and fear.

Sometimes the barrier can be overcome in very simple ways. For instance, an impartial third party might point out objective reality. I have a friend who volunteers his services as a mediator in family and business disputes, and he says that often he does nothing more than referee. The two parties state their problems and what they want, and that's enough to change the subtexts and work out a solution.

Another good method is making a reverse list. It's an offshoot of role reversal, and it can be very effective when a problem arises.

Sal and Norman used it when they ran into a problem in their small business. They were equal partners, but Sal ran the shop and Norman the office. The problems in each place were different, just as the work was different, and from the very beginning neither one could understand the other's problems.

"The trouble is," Norman told Sal, "you don't understand that I can't always order the best equipment, and I can't always give credit to a guy when you promise it."

"Maybe so, but you don't realize it's no picnic running a shop. You promise things too, things I can't deliver."

"You don't understand." "You don't realize." These two expressions are clues to a lack of empathy. A friend who understood this and knew that Sal and Norman had to work together rather than at cross-purposes suggested that each sit down and try to make a list of all the complaints the other had!

Sal did his best to list Norman's grievances, as Norman felt them, and Norman tried to list Sal's complaints. "It made me think," Norman said. "I dug up more reasons than Sal could about how I was bollixing things up!"

"Me too." Sal laughed. "All of a sudden I was finding fault with myself."

It was a beginning, a first step toward empathy, and it worked for them. They were able to understand a little more about each other, enough to break through their problems and cope with them.

A WARNING

While empathy can be a great help in handling other people, too much of it can also be a hazard. I have a friend who started out as a brilliant young neurosurgeon, but after ten years of work in the field, he changed his specialty and started over in hand surgery.

When I asked why he had given up such a promising career, he shrugged. "Promising? Sure. I was good, and I knew it, but I was burned out."

"At your age?"

"That's right. I identified with every patient. I became involved with each one. I was too empathic, too sympathetic, too concerned with their lives. I got to know them, to understand them and feel for them, and if something went wrong I was devastated."

He shook his head. "I just couldn't stand it. No matter how exciting the challenge and work, I had to get out. Look, you don't get that involved with a patient when you're doing hand surgery."

In his case too much empathy, too much sensitivity, had destroyed his ability to send out an authoritative, confident subtext. He couldn't cut back on his empathy, so he changed his work.

TRUTH AND CONSEQUENCES

TO CATCH A LIAR

Tom O'Brian, the chairman and chief executive of the Tremont Savings and Loan Association, had been listening to Jim Nelson, a government representative, for a half hour as Nelson laid out the case against Tremont. At the end of the hard-hitting critique, O'Brian looked Nelson square in the eye and said, "You're right, of course. I tell you what. I intend to resign at the end of this year, and meanwhile I'll do everything I can to untangle the mess."

Later, reporting to his supervisor, Nelson said, "I don't think we should give them the time they asked for. I think we should move in right now. I really think Tremont's investment policies are pure gambles!"

His supervisor frowned. "You think he was lying to you?"

"Absolutely." Nelson hesitated. "Though, to tell you the truth, I don't know why. I can't put my finger on anything he said. He looked me straight in the eye, but . . ." He shook his head. "Maybe I'm wrong. Maybe you should meet with him."

"Me? If you thought he was hiding something, why should I feel any different?"

"I don't know. It was just a gut feeling, but I don't trust him!"

There is no sure way to catch a liar. No single facial expression, no gesture, no element of body language sends out the subtext "I am lying."

If this is so, why was Jim so certain the other man was lying? That "gut feeling" he had was more than intuition. It was a combination of tiny clues to O'Brian's emotions. While there are no definite expressions or gestures that spell out a lie, there are many physical reactions that spell out our emotions. Here are some of them: blushing, sweating, growing pale, or muscle tension.

THE LIE DETECTOR

In our society we like to depend on machines, and to catch a liar, business and the government have turned to the polygraph. We think of the polygraph as a lie detector, a mechanical apparatus that somehow senses when a person is lying. Many businesses depend heavily on the polygraph to keep from hiring the wrong kind of employees.

The great majority of polygraph tests, about 300,000 a year, are given by businesses as part of pre-employment screening to control internal crime and to recommend promotions. In thirty-one states, it is legal to require employees to take a polygraph test. In only eighteen states is it illegal, and even in those states employers can usually find a way around the law. An Office of Technology Assessment report states that to get around the law, employers may tell a worker they suspect him or her of theft, but if innocence can be demonstrated in a polygraph test, the employer will not discharge the employee.

Banks and drugstores, convenience stores, groceries, and fast-food outlets rely heavily on polygraph testing for pre-employment screening. The Justice Department, the FBI, and most police departments use the polygraph after investigators have narrowed down a list of suspects. Many government agencies count on the polygraph for lie detection.

The sad part of all this is that the polygraph is not a lie detector. All it can do is detect changes in our autonomic nervous system: changes in heart rate, blood pressure, skin conductivity, temperature, breathing, sweating, flushing, and blanching—all physical responses that have been linked to emotional arousal.

The theory behind the polygraph is that when we tell a lie, we show a certain amount of emotional arousal. This arousal can be charted by the machine, and the operator can pinpoint which questions caused it—and thus, theoretically, which of the subject's responses are lies.

Unfortunately, there are many problems associated with this technique. The greatest one is that most people can be emotionally aroused by things besides lying. If the question asked by the polygraph operator hits an emotional response, the machine will register it. The emotional response, however, may have nothing to do with lying.

Take the example of a teller being questioned because his or her drawer shows a shortage of five hundred dollars. The operator will start by asking innocuous questions. "Do you live in town?" "Are you married?" "Is this Monday?" And then the casual question is inserted: "Did you embezzle the five hundred dollars?" If the polygraph records emotional arousal at this point, the teller's "No!" can be considered a lie. The obvious flaw is that in all probability any reference to the money will cause an emotional reaction.

The other flaw in polygraph testing comes when the person being questioned is an accomplished liar who has learned to control his or her emotional response—and many people can do that. Another problem is the liar who believes the lie. No amount of testing will shake him or her, because in that person's mind it is not a lie.

THE LYING NURSES

If there are no specific facial or body subtexts to lying, how are we to tell a lie from the truth? Can we? Well, not always, but sometimes we can. There are times when we are absolutely certain that someone is lying, and those are times when the lie is tied to a strong emotion. In a sense, we act as the polygraph does. We link the sudden emotion to the statement, and our inner self cries out "A lie!"

The face is a reliable index to many basic emotions. Dr. Paul Ekman, a professor of psychology at the University of California in San Francisco, conducted a study to find out if the face can give clues to when someone is lying.

He had female student nurses watch various films. Some of the films were pleasant, while others were horrifying medical films in which a burn victim suffered in agony. The nurses were then asked to describe a disturbing film to an interviewer, but to do so dishonestly, to lie about it and say it was enjoyable. They were also asked to describe an innocuous film as distressing.

The purpose of the experiment was to discover whether the interviewer could read anything in the nurses' expressions that would be a clue to lying. Hidden videotape cameras documented the interviews. Nurses were chosen because they were highly motivated to learn how to avoid reacting to body mutilation.

Some nurses were good at lying, some lied imperfectly, and some couldn't lie at all. The poor liars showed fewer of the gestures that usually accompany speech—pointing, drawing pictures in the air, indicating direction and size. Instead they licked their lips, rubbed their eyes, and made nervous motions.

Good liars could fake innocence, anger, or joy, but they still didn't know just when to make these emotions appear on their faces or how long to keep them there and when to let them go.

Distress, worry, or grief often troubled the lying nurses, and these emotions could be detected by the lifting of just the inner part of the eyebrows. The result is a pair of slanting eyebrows raised at the center, a sort of inverted V. The upper eyelids were also pulled up. This combination of movements can only be suppressed voluntarily by one in ten people. In most cases it occurs in spite of efforts to conceal the emotions.

THE TELLTALE SMILE

A clue to lying can come from the way emotions leak through expressions or gestures. The simplest facial expression is a smile, and this is the one most researchers have zeroed in on. But the smile is disappointing because people smile as often when they lie as when they tell the truth.

There are, however, dozens of different kinds of smiles. Dr. Ekman has measured, catalogued, and studied the different types of smiles and has concluded that they are probably the most underrated facial expressions, and that they are far more complicated than people realize.

People smile when they are pleased, happy, content, amused, enjoying life; but they also smile when they are miserable or sad. There are false smiles used like masks that send a subtext that the wearer isn't being entirely truthful.

Dr. Ekman lists eighteen smiles that are not deceptive. These are smiles that are really felt by the smiler. What distinguishes a felt smile from an artificial one is the fact that in the felt smile no other muscles in the lower part of the face are involved. In the upper face, the action that accompanies a felt smile is the tightening of the muscles that circle the eye. This smile lasts longer than a false smile and is more intense when the emotion that causes it is extreme.

We may not consciously be aware of these subtle changes, but they send out a subtext on an unconscious level. Literature is filled with references to false smiles: "He smiled with his lips but not his eyes," or "The smile never reached her eyes." Writers have used these expressions to the point of cliché to distinguish a genuine smile from a false one. This lack of involvement of the muscles around the eye, Dr. Ekman stresses, "is a subtle cue, but a crucial one for distinguishing felt from false smiles."

Consider now a few smiles that are felt, but do not transmit positive emotions. Sometimes we smile when we are afraid. In the fear smile, the lips are stretched to form a rectangular shape. Muscles that pull the lips horizontally in fear will sometimes lift the corners of the mouth in the mockery of a smile, what we call a grimace. In this smile, the eyebrows are raised and pulled together and the eyes are widened.

Another negative but felt smile is one that shows contempt. The corners of the lips are tightened, and usually one side is lifted slightly while the eyebrows are slightly raised. In the smile of someone who is miserable, the lower lip is pushed up by the chin muscle and the corners of the mouth are pulled down. The brows are lowered.

These are a few of the real or felt smiles we use. A false smile, on the other hand, is often used as a mask to hide what one is really feeling. In this smile, the person tends to press the lips together, tighten the corners, and push up the lower lip.

A false smile, according to Dr. Ekman, is often asymmetrical (although some normal smiles are lopsided, too). Only one side of the mouth is involved, and it isn't accompanied by any movement of the muscles around the eyes. Another crucial cue is timing. False smiles may end abruptly or decrease in steps, but in either case the timing is inappropriate.

To sum up the facts about false smiles:

- In pretending fear or sadness, there is no accompanying forehead expression.
- In pretending happiness, the eye muscles are not involved.
- To discover pretense in any emotion, look for asymmetrical expressions, too abrupt an onset of the smile, and an inappropriate length of time for the smile.

MICROEXPRESSIONS

Perhaps the most tantalizing way in which real subtexts are leaked out through facial expressions is those fleeting images that psychologists call microexpressions. They are so fleeting, in fact, that in ordinary talk they are missed entirely. However, they do have a subliminal impact. I remember an incident that occurred while shooting a movie for a drug company. We had set up a camera behind a one-way mirror to film in the doctor's office. The drug in question was a tranquilizer, and we did a series of shots, over a period of a month, while the doctor interviewed patients before and after taking the tranquilizer.

The patients, of course, were told of the filmed interviews, and most of them readily gave us permission to use them. In one interview, a young man, after a week on the drug, told the doctor that he was doing very well, very well indeed.

"I don't believe him for a minute," the cameraman whispered to me, and he was right. Two days later the young man was back in the doctor's office, sobbing hysterically.

"I never suspected it," the doctor told us miserably. "He seemed so cheerful, so convinced his troubles were behind him. You guys saw the interview. What did you think?"

We assured him that we, too, were convinced by his patient, but I remembered the cameraman's disbelief. What had he seen in the patient's manner or heard in his voice?

When alone, I replayed the film of the interview. Watching the young man instead of the doctor, I, too, felt uneasy. But why? On a hunch, I ran the film in slow motion, and then I caught it. Three times, in the course of the interview, while the patient assured the doctor that he was all right, his face dissolved into a heartbreaking expression of sadness—an expression so fleeting, so brief, that at normal speed it went unnoticed.

This microexpression gave the lie to all his words. The cameraman at the time of the interview had noticed it subliminally without understanding what he saw. The doctor, concentrating on the patient's chart, had missed it completely.

When I told a friend, a psychoanalyst, about this, she nodded. "Yes, it impressed you subliminally, but with practice and training you can learn to see those expressions. I've learned because in my practice they are giveaways. In fact, it's one good reason, I believe, for facing a patient during a psychoanalytic session."

Dr. Ekman suggests that one way of training the eye to observe microexpressions and read their subtexts is to have someone flash a photograph of a facial expression as fast as he or she can in front of your eyes. Try to guess what emotion was shown in the picture, then study the picture to confirm your guess. Then try another picture. To become proficient, repeat the exercise with at least a hundred pictures.

Not only sadness leaks through in these microexpressions, but also glee or triumph or cunning—any one of a dozen emotions can be revealed. Matched against the statements being made, they are an intriguing way to catch a lie.

One interesting point about these microexpressions that "leak out" when we are talking is that many of them are not easy to control or fake. They involve certain muscle movements that very few people can make intentionally. But they do make them unconsciously.

As an example, Dr. Ekman says only 10 percent of the people he tested could deliberately pull the corners of their lips down without moving their chin muscles. Yet those he tested, when they felt sadness, sorrow, or grief, did do it!

THE SECRET IN THE EYES

In a New York City department store, a young Hispanic girl was fired because the manager suspected her of pilfering. "She wouldn't meet my eyes when I questioned her," he told a union representative who came to her defense. "I knew she was lying."

The representative, himself Hispanic, shook his head. "What you don't understand," he explained, "is that a well-bred Hispanic girl will not make eye contact with a man who is not a relative. It's just considered too bold. If she's well brought up, she'll look away or drop her eyes."

An error was averted thanks to the representative's good sense, but most people believe the eyes can betray the truth. How many parents have told their children, "Look me in the eye and I'll know if you're lying?" Unfortunately for lie catchers, the eye test is not foolproof. We avert our eyes and refuse to make eye contact for a number of reasons. Social propriety, as in the above example, is one. We may look down with sadness, down or away with shame, and away with disgust.

A liar, however, if at all accomplished, will meet the eyes of the person he or she is talking to with a clear-eyed, steady gaze. As a child, I learned quickly that in order to lie proficiently to adults all I had to do was stare them in the eye. My clear, innocent gaze assured them that I was telling the truth, no matter how big my lie was.

It is, indeed, very easy to control the direction of your gaze. It is harder to control blinking. You can blink voluntarily, but it is also an involuntary act when you are emotionally aroused. Here is a physiological clue you can pick up just as the polygraph picks up excitation. However, it is still only a clue to emotional arousal, not necessarily to lying.

There is still another clue that can give away excitement or joy: the dilation or constriction of the pupil of the eye. This is something beyond our conscious control. It is often very difficult to tell if another person's pupil is large or small unless he or she has blue or gray eyes, but on a subconscious level we are aware of eye pupil changes, and we respond to those changes.

Dr. Ekhard Hess, a psychologist, has spent a great deal of time studying involuntary changes in pupil size, and he has developed a field of study he calls pupillometry. Dr. Hess noticed a correlation between people's pupil size and their emotional response. He found a wide range of responses. When we are emotionally aroused, our pupils widen. When we are displeased, they close. It is a subtle reaction, yet the subtext of the pupil size is understood subliminally. It is another clue when matched against the spoken word.

A final clue to emotion found in the eye is the presence of tears. Tears are usually a clear indication of emotional excitement, although some people can cry on demand. Tears are not always a sign of sadness. They can send a subtext of anger, relief, distress, and even enjoyment.

TRUE OR FALSE

What becomes very clear is that we can only detect a lie by noting the signs of any emotional disturbance the lie causes. These are usually due to changes in the autonomic nervous system. This part of our nervous system also controls our blood vessels. When our blood vessels expand, we blush; when they contract, we grow pale. Neither of these acts is controlled consciously. They happen without our willing them or even wanting them to occur. Someone who blushes may be embarrassed, or ashamed. Someone who grows pale may be frightened or angry. In either case the reaction could be because the person is telling a lie.

Sweating is another physiological process controlled by the nervous system, and while it is often a reaction to excessive heat or exertion, it can also occur when someone is put under emotional pressure.

Other facial expressions may help in detecting a lie. The most common is an "unmatched" face. In this, the same expression appears on both sides of the face, but it is stronger on one side. These unmatched expressions, according to scientists, are clues to the fact that the feeling expressed is fake.

Crooked or asymmetrical expressions, however, are still not a definite clue to lying. Like other clues, asymmetry is only one element in the arsenal needed to judge a possible liar.

Another element in catching a liar is time. How long does an expression last and how long does it take to appear and disappear? According to Dr. Ekman's studies, expressions that last a long time, between five and ten seconds, are probably false and the subtext they send out is not to be trusted. An expression of true feeling is much shorter. Genuine emotions only remain on the face for a few seconds. For instance, to be genuine, an expression of surprise must last less than a second. It must be a fleeting thing.

Everyone, Dr. Ekman insists, is able to produce some kind of false emotion, but a liar has trouble with timing. If an expression of anger comes *after* angry words, it is probably false. Usually a show of genuine anger comes at the start of angry words or even a few seconds before.

The same is true of body language symbols of anger. If an employer bangs a fist on the table to show anger and then vents that anger in words after the fist banging, it is probably false anger. There should also be a synchronization between the facial and the body expression of anger. If they don't match, then you know something is wrong.

THE METHOD AND THE MASK

Although perceiving these elements can help you detect a lie, no clue to deceit in face, voice, words, or body language is foolproof. The people who can lie the best and get away with it often use a technique similar to the Stanislavsky school of acting. They find a situation within their own past experience, either of joy, sadness, honesty, or anything else that matches the lie, and they bring it up to the present so it colors how they feel, and that feeling goes into the lie.

Using that technique, they have found the emotional material to match the lie, and there is less chance that any true feelings will show. In one sense they believe the lie—or at least the feelings that should accompany the lie. In a sense, they are similar to pathological liars, who believe their own lies.

For the liar who cannot use the Stanislavsky method and can't believe the lie, the best way to make sure the truth is hidden is to use some sort of mask. The best mask is a false emotion, and the expression used most often is a smile.

I once worked for a CEO who was going through some serious medical problems at the same time the company was in the midst of important negotiations. The CEO realized that he didn't dare show his physical weakness or that he was in a great deal of pain. As a mask to cover up his real feelings, he smiled constantly. Although there were clues that his smile was false, they weren't picked up by the other negotiators, and he successfully weathered his physical problems without anyone knowing about them.

The best liar sticks close to the truth. He or she never makes up elaborate scenarios. Instead, the liar tells as much of the truth as possible, and then throws in the smallest lie to make the point.

Another technique liars use is to make the truth sound so outrageous that the listener shrugs it off as a lie. An executive seen at lunch with the head of a rival firm was confronted by his boss: "Was she trying to recruit you?"

It *was* a recruitment lunch, but instead of protesting, the executive laughed. "Sure, and she offered me three million a year and a three-month vacation." An obviously nonsensical lie, but it served to cut off any further questioning.

GESTURES AND MANIPULATORS

Certain gestures go along with speech. Hands are used to shape a sentence, to draw a picture in space, to strengthen or to deny what we say. Some cultures, as was noted earlier, use more hand gestures than others; some are very limited in gestures.

An important clue to lying is the rate at which gestures are made. We increase the number of gestures we make when someone doesn't understand us, or when we are angry, upset, or excited. We use fewer gestures when we are uncertain about what we are saying, or when we are repeating a talk for the third or fourth time.

Gestures also decrease when we are cautious about what we are saying.

We may be cautious when what we are saying is important, when we want to make a good first impression, or in many other situations, including lying. If we are not practiced liars, if our lie is not rehearsed, or if the lie summons up strong emotions, our gestures will decrease. However, the person hoping to catch a lie must first know how the suspected liar uses gestures and whether or not he or she is uncertain about other things besides the possible lie.

Dr. Ekman mentions still other possible giveaways in lie detection. There are moments in which a hand grooms, massages, picks, scratches, or in some way manipulates some part of the body. He calls these motions manipulators. They may last only a short time, or they may go on for many minutes. In some people the hair is smoothed, the ear is picked, or the body is scratched. Sometimes the lie evidences itself as hair twisting, foot tapping, finger rubbing, or any kind of nervous fidgeting.

These restless movements are usually made when someone is ill at ease—or lying. There is some question about this because when the stakes are high, when the lie is important, the manipulations may, in fact, decrease. This happens because the liar realizes that nervous fidgeting is considered a giveaway of deception. But in everyday lies, manipulators tend to increase, and the subtext sent out is "this person is lying."

In sum, there are no definite signs, signals, facial expressions, or gestures that will absolutely expose a liar. But there are many little clues to emotional excitement, which is often, though not always, linked to lying.

Schopenhauer gave this advice about catching a liar: "If you have reason to suspect that a person is telling you a lie, look as though you believe every word he said. This will give him courage to go on; he will become more vehement in his assertions and in the end betray himself."

8

ASPECTS OF POWER

THE MAN WHO MISUNDERSTOOD POWER

"This job," my friend Pete told me, "is one I really want, and by God I'm going to get it. I'm really primed for success at tomorrow's interview!"

The job was right up Pete's alley, working with a Computer-Aided Design and Drafting (CADD) program. He knew computers and was just one year away from his engineering degree.

"I've done my homework," Pete assured me.

I assumed he had taken a refresher course in CADD, but no, as he explained it, "The job interview these days is a duel for power. I've studied up on it. I've read *Power Through Clothes, Looking Out for Yourself, Go for Success.* I've read all the books and I'll knock them dead tomorrow!"

I ran into Pete a week later, and I asked, "Did you get the job?"

Pete sighed deeply. "I don't know. I went to so much trouble— I wore a perfectly tailored suit, single breasted with a vest, charcoal gray, and a white shirt. White's always good, the books say. I wanted to appear conservative, send a message of dignity, strength."

"I get it. You dressed for success."

"Exactly. Even wore a maroon tie."

"Looking like that," I said carefully, "how could you miss?"

He looked at me bleakly. "I walked into the boss's office for the interview, and what do you think he was wearing?"

I nodded. "Of course. The same outfit? Or was he dressed for more power?"

"No way! He was wearing running shoes and jeans and a T-shirt! And he was swinging a golf club. Kept fiddling with it all during the interview."

I shook my head. "Really?"

"I took the position of power when we sat down," Pete said wistfully.

"What's that?"

"A firm seat, erect and quiet. Fidgeting betrays an inner weakness, so I sat stiff, my eyes fixed on his. Firm eye contact, you know. It's always supposed to work."

"Did it?"

Pete shrugged. "He kept fidgeting with that golf club. He just ignored my clothes. What a disappointment."

"What now, Pete?"

"Well . . ." He chewed his lip. "I just picked up this book on power through intimidation. Next time I might try a navy blue suit and a yellow tie . . ."

Poor Pete. He had a simple problem. He didn't really understand what power is. He assumed that the subtext of power was power itself. He had read that powerful men dress in a certain way, and he made the false assumption that dressing that way would give him power.

Power, however, is a more subtle thing than the way you dress, the way you move or sit. Pete was thrown off course when he ran up against one of those rare men who are uninterested in the trappings of power that Pete expected.

The boss who interviewed him had enough power to disregard all outward appearances. He could dress as he pleased, act as he pleased, fidget when he wanted to. There was no way Pete could play any power games with a man like that.

The only power Pete had was his knowledge of CADD. This "power" eventually got him an excellent job. He had left his résumé with the boss's secretary, and she sent it on to personnel. There his strength was recognized, and he was called back for another interview.

"Forget what you read about power," I advised him. "Just be straightforward and don't play games."

"Are you sure I shouldn't try a navy blue suit and a yellow tie?"

"Do you want the job, Pete?"

"You know I do."

"Are you good at CADD?"

"Tops."

"Okay, here's some good advice. Sell all those books on power and buy some clothes bags and mothballs."

He looked bewildered. "Why?"

"To store away your power clothes. Dress the way you feel most comfortable, in good taste of course. The guy who interviews you has more power than you. Concentrate on one thing. Your skill at CADD."

"You think that'll work?"

"It'll work better than your other attempt." And I was right. Pete got the job and is happy doing the work he knows best.

THE OLD GAME PLAYER

The word *power* is thrown around pretty loosely, and many of us, like Pete, confuse power with its subtexts. *Webster* does define power as "a possession of control, authority, or influence over others." But the second definition is "ability to get or produce an effect."

It is this definition, the ability to act, that real power is all about. Pete's power lies in his ability at CADD. It was a talent that gave him a unique strength. But the kind of power that Pete had read about in many of the "how to" books was the power that concerns itself with influence, control, or sway.

Baron John Acton, who lived during the second half of the nineteenth century, explained the trouble with this first definition of power when he wrote, "Power tends to corrupt, and absolute power corrupts absolutely." Often, in the business world, this corrupting tendency of power takes the form of obnoxious game playing.

I worked for a boss in a small company who was fond of these power games. We called one of his favorite games "blotting out the light." He would come up to a worker's desk and just stand there. As one young woman put it, "He blotted out the light. He loomed over me like some enormous bird of prey, not saying anything, just looking. If I was on the phone, no matter with whom, I'd have to mutter 'I'll call you back,' and hang up to give him my full attention."

He had another favorite game which Bill, one of the salesmen, labeled "nobody's home on the telephone." As Bill explained it: "He'd call me when he knew I was out to lunch, and he'd leave a message with my secretary. When I tried to call him back, he'd always be in conference.

"I'd leave word that I had called, and sure enough he'd get back when he knew I was away from my desk. He must have clocked every move I made. I'd return the call, and he was 'unavailable' just then.

"This would go on for days, it seemed, and if I met him in the hall and tried to ask what he wanted or set up a date, he'd hurry past in annoyance. 'Why don't you give me a call, Bill.' It wore me down!"

Bill, however, didn't take the game playing for long. He was a good salesman, and that gave him some power. He looked around quietly and found a better job. "I did that while I was still working for the old game player," he told me. "The next time I called him back, and he was 'not available,' I told his secretary, 'Well, he knows where to find me!' "

I laughed, envisioning the boss's face when he heard that. "What did he do?"

Bill shrugged. "Funny thing. He must have realized I didn't care. He did an about-face and became very respectful. I realized then that he needed me, and if I wanted to, I could make some headway."

"Did you?"

"No." Bill shook his head. "I don't like to play those games. I gave him notice and I started the new job the next week."

OF TIME AND THE TELEPHONE

Bill was lucky he had the power to go out and find another job. Many people don't, and have to learn how to cope with the power players—to fight back or submit. There are any number of power plays going on in the workplace. One common ploy is to manipulate time. How you deal with time can send out a strong subtext.

In the United States, a wait of five minutes to see someone on business when you have an appointment is considered normal. If someone keeps a client waiting beyond ten minutes, the subtext is clear—"My time is valuable."

Fifteen minutes, and the subtext is "I am more important than you." Twenty minutes and the subtext becomes "I am contemptuous of you!" A half hour and it is "You are an annoyance. I am seeing you only because I must." Thirty to forty minutes is an unusual length of time to keep anyone waiting. It carries a plain and not-so-nice subtext—"I think very little of you. Your time is unimportant."

On the other hand, when someone comes out as soon as a client is announced and ushers the client into the office, the subtext is "You are a very important person. Your time is more valuable than mine or just as valuable."

These times and their relationship to subtext are a part of our culture. In a Latin culture, by contrast, one may be kept waiting forty-five minutes without its seeming excessive. In some parts of the Middle East, appointments made beyond a week ahead tend to slip into a hazy future and are often forgotten. If you show up for an appointment that is not kept, the other party may not understand your annoyance or the subtext you derive from being stood up. When North American businessmen do business in different cultures, they must understand these cultures' different concepts of time and realize how their subtexts differ from ours.

Understanding the subtexts of time and waiting allows you to manipulate and insult the other person without saying an insulting word. It also allows you to show respect. In our society, the amount of time you keep someone waiting is directly proportional to your perception of that person's status.

Another subtle subtext of power comes through on the telephone. How long does it take you to return a phone call? Do you return the call at all? The telephone can be used in subtle and not so subtle power ploys. When you meet with a client and the meeting is interrupted by frequent phone calls, the subtext can be "I'm an important person." It's a dangerous ploy because it can easily end up annoying the client.

I once worked with a man who would call a colleague into his office for a meeting and always manage to be on the phone when the other arrived. He would wave the colleague to a seat, smile apologetically, and then keep nodding to the phone for another five minutes. His colleague would get the subtext: "I'm such a busy guy, I haven't a moment to myself."

While these games are usually played by people jockeying for position in the business world, there are many people in power who do not abuse their strength, who treat their subordinates decently, and who don't allow themselves to be drawn into power games.

What is it that differentiates people who seem able to handle power and don't have to rely on artificial subtexts from those who can't handle it and must constantly bolster their images? One possible answer may come out of an ongoing study being conducted by a team of young sociologists at a major university.

"We've been studying people who are unable to handle power comfortably," the senior researcher told me. "We do personality profiles on them, and match the results against the profiles of other people who have no trouble with power."

"What have you found out?" I asked.

"It's too early for any firm results, but preliminary results seem to show that people who handle power wisely are more secure in their personalities, better able to cope with life in general."

"I think I could have figured that out from observation alone," I said.

"Sure you could, but we want scientific validation."

Even if his research assures him that secure people are better equipped to handle power, it will not lessen power's attraction to the insecure.

YOUR POWER PROFILE

There is nothing wrong with wanting power. Some people have a need for it, and are able to handle it. If you want power and you need it, how do you go about getting it?

The question of whether you go for power in any situation is a deeply personal one, and the answer must be based on your individual power motivation, your own power profile.

There are guidelines that can help you to determine your power profile. They can help you to discover what direction to take in terms of power: Will you be content to be a follower? Should you strive to become a leader? Or should you stay independent and neutral?

Here is a test that can aid you in understanding your own relationship to power covering four elements. Try to answer the questions by putting yourself in each situation and as honestly as possible decide how you would react.

INTERIOR OR EXTERIOR

People who are uncomfortable with power tend to be interior people. Usually they are creative, no matter what their field, and often they are self-sufficient, able to spend time alone.

Exterior people are more practical. They are very comfortable with other people, and like to manage other people. They can also handle power well, are comfortable with it, and usually desire it.

The first step in discovering your power profile is to find out whether you are an interior or exterior person. Answering the following questions will give you some insight into your own personality, whether you should go after power or whether you'd be ill advised to try. Read each situation and the three possible solutions, then pick the answer with which you feel most at ease.

Love and Marriage

It's that time of life. You have a good job and some direction to your life. The singles scene is out. Time to settle down. What kind of a mate do you want?

(A) He or she has to be perfect: good-looking, talented, interesting, with excellent taste and background. Someone who'll turn you on—and on!

(B) Good-looking? Sure, and at least as smart as you, but, above all, someone you can get along with.

(C) Looks? Character? Okay, but first, someone who can help you out, an asset. Good earning power doesn't hurt. It's as easy to fall in love with a rich person as a poor one, but it has to be someone you'll be proud to walk down the street with, someone with class, someone everyone will envy.

Where to Live

You've been shown a number of apartments. The latest is large, roomy, with high ceilings, and a working fireplace. However, the windows are old and warped, the plumbing is poor, and the kitchen inefficient. The carpeting needs replacing, but the rent is low and the neighborhood is very good.

(A) You take the apartment without much hesitation. The view alone is worth the money, and the high ceilings lend it grandeur. The real clincher is the fireplace.

(B) Sure, the view, the fireplace, and the high ceilings are great, but let's consider the expense—the floor, the plumbing, and the kitchen. What will it take to get it in order? You want to consider the pros and cons before you rush into signing a lease.

(C) It's a good buy in terms of what has to be done balanced against the low rent. You take it. The neighborhood is good and will impress people. The apartment is good for your image, and once it's in shape it will have a classy look.

The Vacation

You and your mate have finally gotten enough cash together for that long-anticipated vacation. The question is, where to go?

(A) You decide on the Club Internationale and their trip to Marrakech and some nearby exotic islands. True, most club members don't speak English, and it's very "pricey," but Marrakech does sound romantic, and those far-off places . . . !

(B) You settle for an island in the West Indies. It's accessible, and the price is right. It has great beaches and few people.

(C) It costs more than you wanted to pay, but you make reservations at the famous White Springs Hotel. All amenities are included—including recreational facilities—so it's a practical place to rest and play. Besides it's "in" this year, and you know some very important people who'll be there.

The Kids

You and your spouse are hitting the thirty mark, and the biological time clock is ticking away. You've spent an evening with some close friends and their new baby, and you come home thoughtful. You decide to talk about passing on your own wonderful genes.

(A) You want a houseful of darling children—or at least five, or else you're very firm about zero population growth, and maybe you should have no kids at all.

(B) Sure, babies are major miracles, and you'll plan for them now. At least two, spaced two years apart.

(C) Well, your friend's baby was a doll, but you don't want to rush into anything. Consider your income and what having a baby will mean to someone in your position.

SCORING

In these few examples, (A) is the approach an interior person is most likely to take. If you tend to go this route, your own emotional reactions are most important to you. Power is something you can do without quite easily.

If most of your answers fall into the (C) category, then you are an exterior person, practical, calculating, and well organized. You probably enjoy power and can handle it.

If, like most people, you fall into the (B) category, then you can go either way, acting as an interior or exterior person depending on the situation. If power comes your way, you can handle it, but the chances are you won't go looking for it.

YOUR DOMINANCE QUOTIENT

Discovering whether you are interior or exterior in personality is only the first step to understanding your own ability to handle power. There are other traits to consider. What is your "dominance quotient," your DQ? What do you know about your need to dominate others? Obviously, if you want to dominate a situation, you also want power. If you don't care about dominance, you usually don't hanker after power. Again, here are different situations with three different types of reactions. Choose the one you'd be most likely to follow.

The Conversation

A group of friends are in the living room talking aimlessly, but still covering some fascinating subjects. You're all relaxed and comfortable.

(A) You listen more often than you talk, and you're sure you're getting a good deal out of the evening. A lot of heavy stuff you were uncertain about now seems clearer. You're really enjoying yourself.

(B) You listen to what the others are saying, but you don't hesitate to put your own views forward. You certainly give as much as you get. You come away feeling you've learned a lot, but you've also opened a few other minds to the truth.

(C) You talk much more than you listen because you have some important things to say about all these matters, and you know the rest will want to hear your side. In fact, you often have to interrupt some irrelevant talk to get your own point across, but it's worth it.

Chow Time

The movie was great, and now the group of you are trying to decide where to go for a good meal.

(A) You listen to all the recommendations, hoping someone will come up with a good suggestion.

(B) You listen to everyone, including the nut who wants to drive twelve miles to this "great diner." Then you suggest that little Italian place that makes its own pasta. In the end, you go along with the one that sounds best.

(C) Never mind those places. You know this terrific charcoal broil spot where the burgers are out of this world. You insist everyone go there because you know they'll love it.

On the Job

Things haven't been going well in your department through no one's fault, and now one of the executives has come up with a wild idea that could really save the day—if it works.

(A) The idea does look good on paper, but if you try it out and it fails, you'll all be up the creek without a paddle. Why take the chance?

(B) It seems like a good plan, and you think it will probably work, but why should you be the fall guy? Put it to a vote and see what everyone thinks. You'll go along with their suggestions.

(C) It's a good plan, and you know it will work. Why not get the credit? You speak up for the plan very strongly and swing the rest to your viewpoint.

SCORING

The scoring here is similar to the interior/exterior test. If you tend to follow the (A) mode, you're the least dominant and probably uncomfortable with power. The (C) type of person is the most dominant, has the highest DQ, and will go after power whenever possible.

The great majority falls into (B). They accept power, but won't go after it. They resist dominance by others, but rarely try to be dominant themselves.

AGGRESSION

Aggression is the third element that determines how comfortable you will be with power. This series of questions should help you to understand your degree of aggression.

The Movie Line

It's supposed to be a great flick, and you've been waiting for weeks for it to come to town. You're on line to get your ticket, and what a line! Clear around the block. Then, when you turn to see just how long the line is, some joker cuts in ahead of you!

(A) You're really ticked off, but you're close enough to the front of the line to get a seat, and why make a fuss? It will just create an uncomfortable situation. Better forget it.

(B) Sure, there are plenty of seats and it probably doesn't make any difference, but why should the jerk get away with it? You don't say anything to him directly, but in a voice that carries you tell the person behind you that bucking the line is a pretty cheap trick, and most civilized people wouldn't do it.

(C) That's some maneuver, you think, and you tap him on the shoulder and say, "Look, I was here first. If you want to buck the line, get in behind me if they'll let you. No way are you cutting me off!"

The Waiter with the Water

You're in a restaurant, and after the waiter takes your order you ask him for a glass of water. He starts serving the meal without getting it, and you ask again. Again he forgets it, and his attitude is very unpleasant. Finally, and gracelessly, he brings the water, but you've quite lost your thirst for it.

(A) You're really burned up by all of this, but who wants to make a scene? You leave a very small tip to show how you feel.
(B) You don't wait for the meal to be served. Once you understand that this waiter is unpleasant and giving you minimal service, you get up and walk out of the restaurant.
(C) You tell the waiter off in no uncertain terms and demand to see the maître d' or the manager, explain the situation, and ask for an apology and another waiter.

The New Neighbors

The empty house next door has finally been sold, and a new family has moved in. They appear to be about your age.
(A) You wait for some natural situation to occur, a situation that will allow you to meet them casually.

(B) You set up a small neighborhood party, and invite the new people with the other neighbors. Afterwards you can all compare notes and see if they're your kind of people.

(C) Once the moving van has gone, and the curtains are up, you walk over with a bottle of wine and introduce yourself and welcome them to the neighborhood.

SCORING

By now you know the principle involved. (C) is a sign of a high degree of aggression. If you feel most comfortable with the (A) solutions, you can be reasonably sure power is not for you. The great number of people fit into the middle, (B). They have an aggressive approach, but it does not dominate their lives. They can handle power, but they don't need it or go after it.

LEADING THE REST

Finally, the fourth quality of power is leadership. People with a drive toward power are happiest leading the flock. However, a personal distaste for leadership doesn't mean knuckling under to the power of others.

The CEO

You are an executive in a large company, and you have just come from a meeting with the CEO. She's outlined goals for the coming year, and as you listen you realize the terrific strain she's under to meet those goals. Alone in your office, you recap the meeting.

(A) This woman has a really tough job, and she's welcome to it! Who needs that kind of pressure? You're happy working on your own level.
(B) There's no doubt the CEO works too hard. Is it all that good for the company? She should relax and let the staff take over some of the pressure.
(C) That's one tough worker, and I feel for her. Someday I'll reach her position and have to go through the same routine. There must be some techniques I could learn now to make things easier for me when that time comes.

The Method

Someone who works under you has come up with a promising but untried method for doing one of the crucial jobs. She sends you a memo about it.

(A) You don't really know whether or not the method will work, so you thank her for the idea and shelve her memo.
(B) The method is interesting, but why take a chance with something new when what you're doing works? Still, if it's promising, others should examine it. You pass it on to the higher-ups.
(C) The method, you realize, may help your department, and also help you. You decide to look into it and perhaps implement it.

The Order

You're working in a large company, and an executive above you gives an order that bothers you. What do you do?

(A) The very fact that the executive is above you indicates that the order is correct, and you carry it out.

(B) You talk over the order with the executive, discuss the pros and cons, and finally agree to carry it out.

(C) You're not at all sure this is the best way to handle the situation. You tell this to the executive. "Now this is the way I would do it . . ."

SCORING

Like the other tests, the (C) reaction is the one that indicates the highest power potential. If it's the way you think you would act, then the indication is that you have good leadership qualities. You're willing to take chances, and you know how to handle people and how to react when you are in charge. The (A) reaction is an indication that you wouldn't be comfortable as a leader. If you fall into the (B) category, you can either take leadership or leave it alone.

The important thing about all these tests and the categories they indicate is that men and women don't come in standard black-and-white models. They are available in all shades of gray. They can have a small drive toward power, a moderate drive, no drive at all, or an overwhelming drive—and they are all prone to change. Sometimes a taste of power shoots one from the (A) to (C) category and to an abuse of it; or someone who has thrived on power may suddenly see it all as an illusion without inner rewards, and may turn from it.

BECOMING A LEADER

It is all well and good to realize that your PQ is high and that you have the potential to be a leader and handle power, but what good does that do you if the opportunity to lead never arises? Is power situational? Does it depend on being in the right place at the right time, or are there some people who can rise above their situation to become powerful—people who will create their own opportunities?

Take a person who scores high in handling power, but works in a subordinate position. If the right circumstances present themselves, she could be a leader, but failing that, is she forever doomed to the subordinate role she holds?

Dr. G. A. Talland reported in the *Journal of Abnormal Social Psychology* that he studied men and women in psychotherapy groups. Did those who exerted power and eventually became leaders do so by sensing the opinion of the group and going along with that opinion? Or were their own ideas close to the ideas of the group?

Neither of these two factors was at work, according to Dr. Talland. Careful observation of group dynamics convinced him that the successful leaders were able to gradually change the group's ideas to fit their own. It was less a case of taking advantage of a situation to become a leader than of changing the situation to fit their need for leadership. They were strongly motivated in terms of power, and although the groups they entered had established leaders of their own, they were still able to take power away from the others and become the new leaders.

TOMMY'S TAKEOVER

This ability to change situations to fit one's need for leadership is something we are either born with or learn very early in life. Take Tommy, a four-year-old who was enrolled in a play group by his working mother. Tommy very quickly became the leader of the group, but then his family moved and a year later, at five, Tommy was put in another play group in mid-session.

For a while Tommy was low man on his new group's totem pole, but instead of accepting this, Tommy studied the situation carefully. By playing with the other children, he learned the schedule of activities; then he gradually began to give orders, to tell the other children what to do—and they obeyed him.

A born leader? A powerful personality? Maybe, but what Tommy actually did was to order the other children to do what they were already doing or what they were going to do next anyway! The chances of their disobeying his orders were slim.

Once he established his right to give these orders and be obeyed, he began to make slight changes in the established routine, to insist that everyone should use red crayons to color a woman's dress and blue crayons for a man's suit, or he would hurry things up: "We have to finish all our work by two o'clock!"

The changes were always simple, things no one cared much about, and gradually Tommy's way was adopted.

Once he had come this far, Tommy took a final step. He announced that he owned certain things in the play group, all the crayon sets, the scissors, the paste pots. But he never monopolized his ownership. He graciously gave each object back to the boy or girl who had had it before Tommy announced his possession. He never took physical possession of any of these things, and everyone who used them continued to use them. But very subtly, the right to use them came to be Tommy's disposition.

By the end of the term Tommy was the undisputed leader of the group. He had managed successfully to take power into his own hands. He made the decisions for the group and gave the orders, real orders now and not simple confirmations of what everyone was doing. Tommy had risen above the situation. He had created his *own* situation to take over power.

The way adults assume and keep power is often similar to the technique Tommy used. Within an organization, adults with the equivalent of Tommy's power drive manipulate their own position and the opinions of others to get control. Workers in subordinate positions who desire power, for example, could either change jobs or find some way in which their strengths could be better used in their current job.

If people are subtle and clever in their manipulations, and if we like them, they send out a subtext of charisma. We are glad to go along with their drive for power. If we don't like them, or if their methods are blatant, the subtext they send out is one of cunning or unscrupulousness. Still, in the end, if we strip away both subtexts, their methods seem to be the same.

9

THE JOB
INTERVIEW

YOU'VE GOT SOMETHING THEY WANT

We've explored some of the basic ways in which subtext is projected and how you can interpret its meaning. Now let's explore how you can use this awareness—and some simple techniques—to keep you a step ahead on your chosen career path.

One situation in which subtext may be vitally important—for both interviewer and interviewee—is the job interview. My first job interview came after I had been married for ten years, had three children, and owned a house in the suburbs. I had been a free-lance writer all that time, but there was nothing reliable about my income, and our third child precipitated the need for a steady wage.

"The problem is," my wife said, looking critically at the only suit I owned, which I always wore for weddings and funerals, "I don't think that's the right thing to wear. What do you wear to a job interview?"

What do I wear? What do I say? Can I tell them I've been free-lancing for ten years? Won't wanting a job now mean I'm a failure? Will they want to hire a failure? And what about a résumé? They had asked me to bring one, but what exactly was a résumé? All I had to show for the last ten years was a collection of books and articles!

My wife calmed me down, decided I should borrow a gray suit from my brother, and told me as I left, "Just remember. They want to hire you. Maybe hundreds of people answered that ad, but you're the one they chose to interview. You've got something they want. Go in with that attitude in mind, and remember, if you don't get the job it's still not the end of the world."

"You've got something they want!" That piece of advice stayed with me throughout the interview, and it allowed me to send out a subtext of relaxed control and confidence. I got the job over a half dozen applicants, and a year later, the man who interviewed me confided that my experience was less than anyone else who applied. "But you could write. We had some of your books and articles, and you seemed so comfortable and at ease during the interview that you impressed me. I thought, this guy doesn't really need the job, but he's very together. That's one reason we hired you."

For me it was a triumph of pretense. I did need the job. I was nervous and anxious and uncertain, but I used the two-hour trip down to Philadelphia, where the interview was, to "psych" myself up with my wife's words, "You've got something they want." It was also my first introduction to the fact that you could send out a subtext completely at variance with what you really felt!

THE RÉSUMÉ AND ITS SUBTEXT

Every job applicant who makes it to an interview has something the employer wants, a skill that can be useful, or else he or she would never have gotten as far as the interview. The résumé eliminates those who are not needed or useful to the firm. Your résumé, therefore, is probably your most persuasive element in your job hunt. Know your résumé intimately, and you'll be able to discuss anything on it.

The first step in any job application, therefore, is the résumé, and the résumé itself sends out a subtext. Make sure the subtext is exactly right for the position you want. For that matter, any company you want to work for will have a subtext of its own. Before you go after a job, before you even send out your résumé, and long before the actual interview takes place, bone up on the company. Learn everything you can about it.

There are many ways to do this. Send for their annual report. For a more honest view, if the company is large enough, ask a stockbroker to get you a brokerage house report. Get to the public library and look the firm up in the *F & S Index of Corporations and Industries* or *The Business Periodical Index*. Know something about the executives you are likely to meet. Browse through *Standard and Poor's Register: Directors and Executives* or *Who's Who in Finance and Industry*.

There are many other sources: trade journals, magazines, company employees, news releases. Any of these may supply you with facts you need to know. The point is, know as much as you can about the company before you walk into the interview, and you'll be able to match your strengths to the job.

All this knowledge can help you to slant your résumé to present a subtext that will appeal to that particular company. While it is obvious that you can't change what you've done, or lie about it, you can, by emphasizing certain aspects of your experience, match the needs of the company.

My own job interview was with a drug company, and although I had never worked for a drug company, I achieved a subtext of medical know-how by emphasizing that I had been a premedical student, had run a medical laboratory in the army, and had written articles about medicine and the biography of a doctor. The company that interviewed me wanted a medical writer, so I also emphasized my writing experience.

WHAT TO WEAR

So you start with your résumé, and it's successful enough to earn you an interview. The next problem is what to wear and what your personal grooming should be. Remember that you will send out some sort of subtext the moment you enter the room. Bear in mind that no matter how "laid back" a company may be in terms of its dress code, none of it applies to the interview.

A personnel assistant for a Texas firm that operates petroleum pipelines assured me, "Even if you're going to wear them on the job, we don't like to see jeans in an interview!"

Dress conservatively if there is the slightest doubt. For women, dresses are suitable, but the safest clothes are tailored blouses, skirts, and jackets. Suits can be fine, also. Don't wear pants. They are just not appropriate at an interview. Once you're hired, pants can be worn if other people on your level or higher wear them.

Avoid bright colors and extremes. No matter what the current style is, a miniskirt is ill advised and so are off-the-shoulder blouses or anything too low-cut. Again, what you might wear on the job is not what you should wear to the interview. Try for muted colors and conservative styling.

Makeup, too, should be muted. Blushers should be played down as much as possible. If lipstick is used, go for a pale shade. Avoid too much eyeliner and mascara, and keep your fingernails short with clear or pale-colored polish.

Jewelry should be minimal, not more than one ring, and a wristwatch is preferable to a bracelet. If worn, earrings should be simple. A necklace should be as plain as possible. You want to project a subtext that says "I am not frivolous. I am a serious worker, capable and sensible."

For men, the old standby of a gray or dark blue suit is best, with dark gray preferable. Avoid black suits at the interview. You should have some idea of your own coloring and what colors are best for you. If you're bewildered about this, as many men are, there are color consultants available, and for a fee you can learn some worthwhile facts about how to dress.

For the interview, shirts should be white and ties pin-dot, rep stripes, or refined foulard designs, the colors muted. Suspenders, if worn, should match the tie in color and, preferably, be completely covered by the jacket.

Men should avoid jewelry. A wedding ring is acceptable, as is a wristwatch. Nothing more. If you wear an earring, take it out for the interview! Shoes should be simple and well polished, socks over the calf and not drooping. Hair should be neat and beard and moustache trimmed.

Beards are pretty well accepted by now, their subtext likely to be serious, even scholarly. Again, it's important to match the subtext your appearance sends out against the job you're after. Even today, there are some firms that frown on beards. A little research should tell you if this is the case.

It hardly seems necessary to stress personal grooming, except that a surprising number of men are not aware of the need for it. Fingernails should be short and clean, hands clean. Remember all those schoolboy lectures about cleanliness and grooming!

THREE ELEMENTS AND THEIR SUBTEXTS

The first impression you make is extremely important. It is possible for someone to like you at "first glance," and interviewers are attracted to people who are well groomed. Aside from your clothes, there are three elements that contribute to the subtext you send out and the first impression you make: the way you look at the interviewer, the way you shake the interviewer's hand, and the way you carry yourself.

Starting with the last one, just walking into the office sends out a quick subtext. Do you stand erect or do you slouch? Do you come forward hesitantly or walk forward purposefully? Your walk can reveal a great deal about you. A slouched posture sends a very definite subtext of depression, of carrying a great weight on your shoulders. An erect carriage sends a subtext of control, a take-charge element.

Eye contact: This has been discussed in previous chapters, but it bears repeating. Look your interviewer in the eye at the very beginning, and maintain eye contact throughout the interview. This does not mean a steady, unbroken, and unnerving stare. Break eye contact frequently, but do come back to it. This is the way to send out an honest and forthright subtext.

As for the handshake, it should be full and firm. By full, I mean giving the entire hand in a shake, not just the fingers. There is nothing as off-putting as a limp shake. Its subtext is "I don't want to become involved with you." This is no message for a job interview!

A man's handshake should be firm without being bone crushing and macho. The point of a handshake is contact, not a battle of wills. The macho handshake sends a subtext of an aggressive desire to compete, and is absolutely out of place in a job interview!

Women sometimes have difficulty with the handshake—understandable since the shake involves body contact, and so much subtext can be transmitted by it. A man holding a woman's hand for too long sends a subtext of intimacy, usually a disturbing one. Occasionally, the handshake is not offered to a woman applicant, a sign that the interviewer is confused about the subtext of the shake. Since having your hand extended with no response from the other person gives you a feeling of humiliation, however slight, let the interviewer initiate the handshake.

A woman's handshake should be full, firm, and brief. Inevitably, in a job interview, you will run up against an interviewer who violates all the rules of shaking hands, perhaps giving only the fingers in a limp fashion or giving too hearty and heavy a shake.

This can be an advantage to the applicant because it usually indicates that the interviewer is new at the game.

THE BEGINNING OF THE INTERVIEW

The second stage of the interview is how you sit and the subtext sent out by your posture—and you do sit for the interview. Standing and looming over an interviewer's desk is foolish and threatening. The interviewer should always be in charge, or at least think that he or she is.

Stanly Hyman, a career counselor, coaches job applicants in what he calls nonverbal, physical mannerisms that he claims can send a subtext of assertiveness and control in the first few minutes of an interview.

He advises that you place your chair at a forty-five-degree angle to the interviewer's desk so that you are almost sitting sideways to it. When you sit down, cross your legs toward the interviewer to indicate strength, and open your jacket to show you're secure. Pull down your jacket collar so that it's tight up against your shirt to keep your suit from looking ill fitting.

Place your elbow on the chair arm nearest the desk, and lean a bit on it, Hyman says. Never put your hands together. That means you're trying to control yourself. If the interviewer tilts backward, you back off, too—otherwise you'll scare him (or her). Now you can proceed comfortably with the interview.

There is some value in this advice, but the applicant should not be that concerned with all the small details of maneuvers that Hyman advises. Sit up straight, of course, but be relaxed. Don't hold your hands together—it's a little-boy or -girl posture— and in most situations, lean into the interview. Leaning back is a bit too relaxed a posture. It sends a subtext of "I don't want to get involved."

Avoid nervous gestures, playing with a pen or pencil or any other object, tapping the feet, drumming the fingers. A certain amount of nervous tension is inevitable and even beneficial. It will keep you on your toes, alert and wary, but don't express yourself in nervous, repetitive gestures.

THE RUG AND JUG RULE

A member of the Los Angeles Management Counselors Association suggests that before you reach the office where the interview takes place, you should study the subtext of the company that is interviewing you. You can pick up clues from the surroundings as to what sort of firm it is. If the company is in the country or suburbs, notice the condition of the building. Are there weeds growing in front of it? Are the grounds well kept? Are the buildings properly maintained? In the city, see what sort of building the offices are in. Are you treated indifferently by the receptionist, or does he or she act as if you were expected?

What sort of attitude is there among the employees? While you are waiting, see if the receptionist feels free to chat with you as well as with other employees. A general rule of thumb is that if the subtext of the buildings, offices, housekeeping, and employees is good, the odds are that business is good, too.

The president of a well-known career-planning agency suggests that "the job level of the manager who interviews you may be indicated by whether he or she has a rug on the floor and a water jug on the desk. Most big corporations have a rug-and-jug rule. If that person has to make do with vinyl and goes to the drinking fountain, it's an indication of how prestigious your own job will be!"

Of course there may not be an actual rug on the floor or a water jug on the desk, but the principle applies: How well furnished is the interviewer's office?

The interview itself is, to be sure, more important than all the physical elements of body language and image projection that surround it. I asked the head of personnel at a large company what was the bottom line on advice to a job candidate at an interview. "Two words. Keep cool," was the response. "What applicants forget, because they're so involved with how they should look and act, is that the interviewer is a person, too, and, like you, under pressure. Interviewers don't like to waste time.

"The very fact that you have an appointment is a sign that the interviewer thinks you can do the job. The interview gives the interviewer a chance to explore the things that don't go into a résumé, the personal characteristics and the subtext beneath the surface.

"What you must remember is that an interview goes both ways. It gives you an opportunity to find out something about the company, something that won't be available anywhere else."

THREE TYPES OF QUESTIONS

Another personnel director suggests that in any interview there are three types of questions. Listed below are the types and samples of some of these questions.

Opportunity questions:

- What do you see yourself doing five years from now?
- Tell me about yourself.

- What personal accomplishments have given you the most satisfaction?

Questions like those above give you the opportunity to take charge of the interview.

Threatening questions:

- Do you feel you can handle this job?
- Why did you leave your last job?
- What makes you think you can handle this job without direct experience?

You can handle threatening questions by assertive, moderate-risk answers. Express your competence, but try not to antagonize the interviewer.

Neutral questions:

- Who was your last employer?
- Have you had much experience with this work?

These pose no threat and give you a chance to expand on your background.

Another personnel director says the best way to handle an interview is to walk a middle line. "Follow the lead that's given to you by the interviewer, but watch for a chance to take control of the interview. Be sure your questions get to the point. Don't ramble when you answer questions. Ask about the business and its needs, but stay away from pension plans and retirement benefits. These will be laid out by the interviewer if he's doing his job properly."

Shifting the focus of the interview so that you are the one asking questions is a good idea. For one thing, it puts the interviewer at ease. Most interviewers are bound to be a bit nervous even if they have been in personnel work for a long time. A good opening question is "What kind of person are you looking for?" This buys you time to relax and gives you some insight into the company.

I asked just this question in my first job interview. The answer was a surprise. The interviewer leaned back and, looking up at the ceiling, said, "We're looking for someone a little far out, someone who can write but hasn't been in the medical field before. We want fresh ideas."

That reply threw me for a moment, but luckily I rallied and took the chance to explain my own credentials as a free-lance writer, as well as to talk about some projects I had worked on but had left out of my résumé as too unusual. I had been nervous about those projects until that moment. Now I realized why they were interviewing *me*, a person with no real experience in the field, and I relaxed. No need for pretense any longer!

When you do answer questions, stress your strong points in relation to the job, not your weaknesses. Watch the interviewer and understand his or her subtext. This will clue you in on when to expand on a point and when to cut it short. Watch for lack of interest or genuine interest.

An excellent tool that will give you a clue to the subtext of the interviewer is the head nod. A nodding interviewer means an agreeable one, one who understands you. The head nod is also a clue to expand on what you're saying because you're on the right track.

As a candidate, you have to persuade the interviewer that your abilities mesh with the company's needs. You must sell yourself without sounding as though you're boasting. It may be that you are looking for a better opportunity and are changing jobs of your own accord, but if you were fired and you try to suggest that you were terrific at your last job, the obvious question is "Why were you fired?"

Being fired isn't an obstacle to being hired. Joe Redmond, Pepsico's personnel administrative manager, points out that "people are often fired because the company is cutting back, or there's a personality conflict."

As a precaution against the problem of having been fired, job applicants should try to reach an agreement with the boss who fires them not to send a bad reference. The reverse is also true. Never bad-mouth a former employer. It raises the interviewer's suspicions that you may talk the same way about anyone who hires you.

When it comes to salary, Dudley Darling, a New York executive recruiter, says, "I'd advise the candidate to go for the highest realistic figure. Ask for a 15 to 20 percent raise over your last job, and let the interviewer either meet it or make a counteroffer. If the rest of the interview went well, the chances are the interviewer will meet it."

HANDLING TRICKY QUESTIONS

There are many questions asked in an interview that are designed to trick you or to put you on the defensive. Here are some samples and some suggestions about handling them.

What do you know about our company? If you've done your homework, you can come up with some discussion of products produced, company size and income, company reputation, and its image. Whether or not the question comes up, be prepared to answer it. You want to send out a knowledgeable subtext. Whatever you do, don't try the "I don't know much, but I'd like to learn" approach. It won't get you brownie points. Dig into your research beforehand, and if that fails try to find someone who works for the company who'll talk to you about it.

Why do you want to leave your present job? This presumes that you are still working when you are interviewed. The best answer is that there was no place you could go in the company. Upward mobility is limited, or the work isn't challenging. Perhaps you want a more dynamic company. Another answer might be your salary isn't good enough, and you're after more demanding work with better opportunities.

A good answer here could be that you are after a line job instead of a staff job. Line is sales, marketing, production. Everything else is staff. Line jobs affect profits directly; staff jobs contribute to profits indirectly. They are company overhead and are usually the first area where layoffs occur.

Why did you leave your last job? This question is almost a must for interviews. If possible, try to give a group answer. Some examples: "Our entire division was let go." "After the buyout our territory was cut." "The major suppliers left town."

Defend yourself without being too defensive. A good answer is "I planned for the time to look for a new position and I've put away enough to tide me over."

If you were fired, unless it was for insubordination, nonperformance, or embezzlement, it's not something to be ashamed of, nor is it something that will be held against you. Most people get fired because of a clash in personalities, new management who bring their own people with them, or a cutback that eliminates their job. Whatever the reason, don't be negative about your last boss or company. Try to find an explanation that takes the blame away from you. A few examples: "I went as far as I could go, and there was nothing else open." "My job has been eliminated, and no one is filling it." "They discovered that I was looking outside, and they asked me to leave." The trick is to turn a negative subtext into a positive one.

An important point in answering this question is to know what your references have said about you. One good way to check this out is to have a friend call up your old company, say you are applying for a job, and ask for references. If there are negative elements in your references, try to talk them over with your ex-boss and see if they can be softened. But the best thing to do is to give, as references, people you know will speak well of you.

Your résumé is good, but aren't you overqualified for this job? Don't deny it. You can use this gambit to really sell yourself. Explain that your overqualifications are your employer's good luck. You can do this in a number of ways. One is to show the similarities between your last job and this one, or how your past experience, even if it's from a different field, can be of great value in this job. A point here: every industry has its own lingo. Know the terminology of the business and use it.

What didn't you like about your last job? Give an honest answer to this one, but in a positive sense. Once again, do not speak negatively about your last employer. The subtext you want to send out is that you had more to give to your company than they cared to use. One ploy is that at your last job, seniority meant more than hard work in terms of promotion. You like to work hard.

Another possible answer is that meeting deadlines and schedules is important to you, and you don't think the last job used your strengths, or promotions were too slow and weren't based on performance. Try to answer any question in an interview with a response that sends out a positive subtext, but do it subtly!

What are your strong points? Know at least seven, and try to relate each to the job you are after. The subtext you want to send is: "I am organized, goal oriented, persevering, not rigid, and able to manage and motivate a staff. I work well by myself or as a team member. Before the interview, prepare a list of your strengths. Don't be taken by surprise.

What are your weak points? All of us have them, but in a job interview, while you should be honest about some minor ones, there is no need to give away the store. The point here is to try to make a weakness a plus without being obvious. Send out conflicting subtexts with the positive one the stronger. Here are a few examples: "I'm impatient. By that I mean I'm very result oriented." "I tend to get in and work with my subordinates. It may not be great management, but I like important work done on time." "I hate to do detail work, but I do it thoroughly." You get the point?

FROM THE OTHER SIDE OF THE DESK: WHAT THE INTERVIEWER SHOULD KNOW

As difficult as it may be to be interviewed, it is often more difficult to be the interviewer. You would hesitate to make a major purchase for your company on the basis of one or two meetings with a salesperson, but you are asked to hire an employee after only one or two interviews.

Where the job interview is held is an important part of the

process. As the interviewer, you want a subtext that will establish rapport and encourage the applicant to be relaxed and to talk easily. The best place for an interview is a private office; however, try to use an office that will give you, the interviewer, a subtext of prestige. Remember that you represent the company. If necessary, borrow another office for the interview, one that is upscale.

Dress to display a professional and courteous subtext. Remember that the subtext is not only yours but the company's as well. If the applicant is a man, he will assuredly wear a jacket and tie. If you are a man, wear one too. If you are a woman, dress as the applicant would, neatly and conservatively.

Avoid any distractions during the interview. Arrange to have no phone calls or knocks on the door. Begin by identifying yourself by name and title, then try to put the applicant at ease. Start the talk with something unrelated to the job. Does the applicant have a hobby? Discuss it, or let him or her explain it to you.

However, remember that in the interview the applicant should do the bulk of the talking. Instead of telling the applicant what type of person you are looking for, or trying to sell the company and the job, steer the conversation so that the applicant reveals strengths and weaknesses.

A dangerous point about selling the job is that as the interviewer, you may reveal just what you are looking for in a candidate, and later in the interview, a clever applicant can feed this back to you.

Encourage the applicant to talk openly by sending out a subtext of interest and sympathy. This can be accomplished easily by judicious head nodding at the right moment, or by brief comments: "Uh-huh," or "I can understand that." Or by a smile.

Encourage the candidate to be open by sending out a subtext

of openness. Don't fold your arms. Lean into the interview and try for frequent eye contact.

Active listening is a useful tool. It consists of occasionally restating or rephrasing what the other person has said. The subtext sent out is "I understand what you are saying."

Try not to interrupt the applicant even if you disagree. Avoid jumping in too quickly. Wait for the candidate to finish his or her train of thought. Try to play down the negative aspects of the interview. What you want to do is send a subtext of interest and understanding that will encourage applicants to keep talking and to reveal as much as they can about themselves. Keep your own note taking brief.

Don't worry about pauses in the conversation. Silence can be a useful tool. It can sometimes draw more information as the applicant, feeling uneasy, elaborates on previous statements. The object is to draw as much out of the applicant as you can.

There should be a careful structure to the interview. Although you may want to start by discussing something innocuous, such as hobbies or travel, avoid personal questions at the very beginning. The subtext such questions send out may be disturbing, and sometimes illegal! Start your questions with work experience, then education, and then you can segue into more conversational matters. Delaying the personal history like this gives you a better chance to elicit significant data about the applicant's personal life. If you pose personal questions at the beginning, the applicant will tend to resist, or be guarded.

Always end interviews on a positive note. Compliment the applicants on accomplishments and let them know when you will get back to them about your decision. Remember, above all, that the subtext you project of yourself and your company is just as important as the subtext projected by applicants.

10

THE MAGIC
BEHIND THE
SALE

WILL IT KEEP ME WARM?

Some people are born salespeople and seem instinctively to know all the right moves when it comes to selling, but most of us have to learn the moves. That's not such bad news; almost anyone can learn the elements of selling—and one of the strongest elements is subtext.

A sales executive of a large firm told me, "It boils down to the subtexts of three things: you [the seller], your company, and your product. Each has a subtext, and believe me, the subtext of any one of these three can make or break a sale."

It was another expert, a sales-training specialist for United States Rubber, who, many years ago, explained just what the subtext of a product was. "Too many salespeople," he said, "make the mistake of trying to sell only the product and forget all about the product's subtext." To show what he meant, he told the story of a young heating system salesman who called on an elderly woman. She lived alone in a big house, and she had shown interest in an oil burner. The salesman was a pro and knew his product. For a good hour he lectured this woman on boiler capacity and combustion and all the details of the boiler's construction. He told her everything, and then, rather smugly, asked if there was anything else she wanted to know.

She sighed. "Well, yes. Will it keep an old lady warm?"

The point is, the most vital subtext of any product is not how it is constructed and how intricate it is, not even how long it will last, but simply whether or not it will work. In this case, the woman cut right to the heart of the product's subtext: "Will it keep me warm?"

Actually, the subtext of a product is quite complicated. For any product, subtext is a two-part thing. One part is how well it works: in the case of the heating system, "Will it keep me warm?" The other part is the product's aura. Webster's dictionary defines an aura as a subtle sensory stimulus, and I have used the word very deliberately because an aura has a subtext of its own—a mystical, ethereal subtext.

Every product has an aura about it. Ideally, the aura is related to how well the product works. In the best case, the aura depends on performance. However—and it's a big *however*—the aura can be manipulated by clever advertising so that it has very little to do with the performance of the object being sold.

An example of how advertising attempts to build up an aura unrelated to the object's performance is the 1989 advertising campaign for the Infiniti car. Rather than show the car and describe its good points, the ad shows elements of nature that have clear-cut subtexts: breaking waves, craggy cliffs, sunsets. Then the name of the car is splashed across the TV screen or magazine page.

Never mind what the car looks like or how it runs. Never mind its price or any other features. Performance is of minimal concern here; aura is everything. Or perhaps we should say subtext is everything, for aura, of course, is simply another name for subtext. The advertising campaign for the Infiniti is an attempt to establish the car's aura, or second subtext, from the start.

The auras of prestige cars like the Cadillac, the Rolls-Royce, the Lincoln Continental, the BMW are so well established that we don't need the assurance of performance. The aura stands in for performance, but the aura has been acquired legitimately over years of performance. With the Infiniti, the advertisement is trying to cut out all those years of performance and present us with a full-blown aura for a car we have never heard of.

As another example, take the popular and well-known perfume Chanel. A recent Chanel advertisement doesn't even bother to show the perfume bottle. The ad has a group of attractive women and men gathered around a pool table, all looking vaguely sultry. Above them is the name Chanel. What does it say about the object they are selling? Nothing, really, but it speaks volumes about the aura of Chanel. Ultra-sophisticated people too cool to smile are playing pool. You, too, can be ultra-sophisticated if you use Chanel. This is the aura being sold.

A cosmetic ad for Elizabeth Arden shows an exquisite female

model sitting in a modern chair. Again no mention of product. What are they selling? Is it the aura of the model? Or the aura of the striking design in the ad?

In this case, it may be the aura of the company that produces the object. If the company is strong enough to have a well-established aura, we are conditioned to accept any product it makes: Elizabeth Arden, Bill Blass, Ralph Lauren. To get down to more useful things, the names Electrolux, Hoover, and Whirlpool have each developed an aura whose subtext is dependability and quality.

Maytag, in an attempt to build up a subtext of reliability, doesn't bother to tell us how good their machines are. In their ads they show repairmen who despair because there is no work for them.

Honda attempts the same sales approach in its advertising, trying to create a subtext equal to the big names. Its ads show salespeople who are unhappy because the car sells itself. The trick in all these cases is to send out a subtext of durability and desirability so that we assume their products are the best.

THE SUBTEXT AND THE SELLER

Even when the product and the manufacturer send out solid subtexts of dependability, there remains the subtext of the salesperson. Successful salespeople are those who send out subtexts of honesty, trust, and sincerity.

One of the best salespeople I knew was in real estate. She gave the appearance of being naive, a little confused, always shuffling through her papers to find the right one, and in the process sending out a subtext of guilelessness. She always managed to come up with just the paper she needed, because in reality she had a mind like a steel trap! But her customers trusted her completely. They just knew, after ten minutes with her, that she was incapable of deceit. That subtext of innocence helped her more than all her considerable knowledge of selling.

If at all possible, try to narrow the subtext of what you're selling down to one specific detail. This not only makes the sale easier to deal with, but it also allows you to be more convincing. Very few people are going to believe all the great things you tell them about a product, but they can be convinced of one important thing. If you choose correctly, that one thing will sell the product.

WHEN THE CUSTOMER RESISTS

On the subject of buyer resistance, think carefully before you even approach the buyer. Okay, so the person might have an objection. Pause before you respond to it, even if you know the answer. That pause sends out a subtext to the buyer. It says the objection is registering in your mind. That's of utmost importance. It tells the buyer you're not just sounding off a typical sales pitch, but actually listening to what he or she has to say. It's a classic way of breaking down stubborn resistance. It not only works in sales. It can work in your personal life, too. Everyone appreciates a listener!

The director of sales training for a large West Coast research institute said that the first step in teaching salespeople to handle resistance is to get them to relax. "We teach them to lean back in their chair, not to sit perched expectantly on the edge of it."

At my look of surprise, he explained himself. "The expectant person sends a subtext of 'I'm going to get you at the first chance I have.' He's battle-ready. It's the same subtext as that of the person who stands stiffly erect with arms folded against the chest. What you must understand when you meet resistance, whether in a sale or a presentation, in any aspect of selling, from the front door to the boardroom, is that the average prospect will seldom buy at the end of the presentation, not until he or she is completely satisfied on each point of resistance.

"For this reason, the salesperson has to listen when met with resistance. The subtext sent out must be, 'I'm considering what you say, and I understand it.' The way to do this is by relaxing, by using specific body language signals. Wrinkle your forehead. Frown thoughtfully, nod your head and make eye contact.

"The next step, oddly enough, is to concede. Agree on a broad, general basis. 'I can appreciate your viewpoint,' or 'I know how you feel.' This sends out a disarming subtext because just the opposite, disagreement, is expected. Then, when the prospect is disarmed, try to turn the objection into an advantage and make it the best reason to buy now. This, of course, requires a deep understanding of the product and the customer's needs, but any good salesperson will have all that before the sale starts."

THE FIRST TEN SECONDS

I talked to many people who work in sales while I was preparing this chapter, and the greatest point of agreement I found was the importance of the first ten seconds. All of them urged that salespeople review their voices, their handshakes, posture, and facial expressions to make sure that the first impression is a good one.

One sales executive compared the first ten seconds of a sale to those critical moments when an entertainer walks onto the stage. He had once been a theatrical director, and he pointed out that the "entrance" had been the undoing of many excellent entertainers.

"I had a singer who came to me and said his manager got him tremendous fees, but threatened to let him go if he didn't manage to make more of an impression on the audience. He couldn't figure out what was wrong. I knew it wasn't his voice, so I told him to go to the end of the room and come on stage as if he were before an audience.

"Sure enough, as he walked in he sent out the deadliest subtext possible: an anxious face, no smile, stiff posture—well, we fixed all that and he did well. But my point is that the same thing applies in sales. It's those first ten seconds!"

A young woman who had a great deal of experience in selling on Wall Street, told me about the "three Be's" in her sales approach: be specific, be definite, and be confident.

She said, "I plan my sales talk to be specific, to focus in on one specific part of what I'm selling, and I'm definite in my sales pitch, but above all, I try to project a subtext of confidence. In my business, confidence in my judgment is the be all and the end all!"

"How do you do that?"

"By knowledge. I know my product, my stocks and bonds. I know the market and know the competition. That gives me the ability to project complete confidence. You know, if you don't believe in your product, forget about selling. Get some other job." A good salesperson is convinced herself before she tries to convince others.

That confidence, according to another top-notch salesman, comes from three rules:

(1) Pick the product you like to sell.
(2) Don't ever try to sell a product you don't like.
(3) Don't sell for a company you don't like.

If you violate these rules, your subtext will give you away very quickly!

YOU'RE THE TOP

One aspect of selling is fund-raising. I have a friend who works for a large charitable organization as a fund-raiser. "One of our typical ploys," he confided, "is to find someone interested in our charity and then give him an honorary title and a dinner. You want subtext? The subtext of that maneuver is obvious. We send out invitations in his name to a list of his friends, acquaintances, and business associates. We charge a lot for the dinner, but it's for a charity, so people come, and in addition to the food we offer them some speeches and entertainment."

I frowned. "In effect, you're using him and pressuring his friends."

My friend nodded. "Exactly! You get the point."

"But why would he let you?"

"Why?" My friend shrugged. "For the best reason. Flattery. It massages his ego, and he goes ahead cheerfully."

I hadn't thought of flattery as a selling device, but as I talked to other salespeople, I became aware of how essential a part of sales it could be. "You can please a prospect with a sincere smile," the head of a sales institute told me. "But it's even better to flatter prospects by praising their judgment directly, or by asking for an opinion on some artistic or political matter. The subtext you send with your question is a flattering one. 'You know more than I do.' You value their opinion. Of course, the flattery must be subtle and indirect. In fact, indirect flattery is the best."

I asked how indirect flattery works. "You can use key phrases to compliment and flatter. For example: 'What is your idea? What do you think about this?' People like to be asked for their opinion. Another gambit is, 'I'd like to get some help from you.' The obvious subtext behind that is that the prospect is smarter than you. It's not only flattering, it's disarming. But just be sure, if you use it, you're on the level."

"I've heard a lot about you," is a very effective way to greet a new prospect, but be warned, it must be true. Before you use it, find out enough about the person you're meeting to come back with an answer in that not-so-rare scenario in which the prospect says "Yes? What have you heard?"

A former computer systems salesman I talked to had had experience in direct selling. "I don't do it anymore," he told me with an edge of regret. "I'm sales manager for the company now, but I miss those days. A good day of selling gave me a sense of accomplishment. I got a kick out of it. Flattery? You bet I used it. It got me through the door.

"I'd open with 'My company wants to get your opinion on this software.' I'd never use 'I'd like to take a minute to show you this software.' You see, the first opening asks for advice. It's hard to resist. The second opening invites rejection. I had a whole set of questions like that: 'I'd like you to help us pick out a new direction for next year.' 'Which of these would appeal to most people?' Those are all flattering openings, and the subtext they all send is 'I value your opinion.' You're complimenting them, but you mustn't overdo it. Don't make it too complicated. Don't tell too much. People won't take even a minute to listen to meaningless words.

"Another point about face-to-face selling is that you have to have different approach sentences in case your first one fails, and in the meantime, let your prospect say something, even if it's 'I'm not interested.' When I was selling systems, I'd come back with 'I know you're not interested in this particular software, but I'll bet you are interested in cutting your billing time by seventy percent!' How can anyone say no to that, and it gives you the opening you need."

"What about the blunt refusal?" I asked him.

"I used to hate that," he told me, "but a saleswoman I worked with taught me something about that. She said a straight refusal makes you feel bad, but it works both ways. It makes the prospect feel a bit ashamed and you can use that shame. She told me how, and after that, when I couldn't get in, I'd take one of my cards and write a message on the back, like, 'I'm sorry I interrupted you at a bad time. I should have known you'd be busy. I'm very anxious to tell you about a product that will save you ten thousand dollars a year, and I'll be back tomorrow at such-and-such an hour. I hope you can spare me a few minutes then.' You know, it works. The prospect reads the card, feels a little ashamed about that blunt refusal, and when you come back he or she is usually more receptive."

A QUESTION OF ENERGY

"A key quality of selling," this same salesman told me, "is to put enthusiasm into the product. If you can project a subtext of enthusiasm, you've come halfway to a sale." He, himself, was a short, stocky man with a tremendous amount of energy. Giving me a typical sample sales "pitch," he used visually charged and exciting words to make the quality of the product come across. Listening to him, I could almost see the system in action.

Another thing he stressed was the importance of the physical subtext your approach sends out. "If I shuffled into the office, slouched and tired, the customer I was trying to convince would peg me as just another bored salesman. When I walked in briskly, my head up, he'd figure I had something important to say. All through the selling, my energy level was very crucial."

A saleswoman who specialized in cosmetics talked to me about sales technique. "It's a matter of energy. The customer will sense that energy and react to it. There's a charge in the air, an excitement. I do it with my body. I smile and I move smoothly. I use the energy to project eagerness. My body language talks to the customers. It says 'This won't be boring!' On another level, it says 'use this product and you'll be as energetic and lively as I am!'"

I have heard that same word, *energy*, used by salespeople at all levels, from door-to-door salespeople to corporate managers. It's vitally important in boardroom presentations and in business meetings in general. Trial lawyers claim it can help them manipulate a jury. Energy is one of the most important factors in making a sale. I have been to seminars where after hours of hearing all the different sales techniques and methods the attendees were flagging physically and mentally. Then, in just a few minutes, I would see a seminar leader bring them back to enthusiasm by projecting a subtext of excitement. How? By raising his voice. By adopting a rabble-rousing tone that would charge the air with an electric force. In short, by energizing the room.

When you are enthusiastic, in selling as in any occupation, you excite others. What are the elements that spell out excitement and energy? The first one is movement, movement of your body, your hands, your head. Not random, pointless movement, but controlled movement using all the elements of body language. Done properly, this body movement can project an air of tension and emotional appeal.

If you're in a standing position during your presentation, move about. Don't maintain one posture. Use your hands dramatically to gesture, to point, to shape and project your words. Use your body to open yourself to the prospect. Open arms are effective. Closed arms are deadly. Never fold them in front of you.

An open posture on your part will often elicit an openness from the other person. It's a sort of mirror effect. The openness you elicit will extend to the listener's mind, inspiring a readiness to listen to your pitch.

Use your voice as a selling instrument, not just to project words, but to modulate the timbre and pitch of the sound. Avoid flat, monotonous speech. Raise and lower your voice according to what you are saying. A voice is a magnificent instrument, and it can send out a subtext of excitement as readily as it can a subtext of despair.

But with all this movement, you must still be sure you know what you're doing, that you move your hands properly. The hands are expressive, but they can express the wrong thing. There are a few don'ts you must be aware of:

- Don't be a nose puller. Yanking and pulling at your nose is a nervous affliction and looks bad.
- Don't be an ear twister. This is another nervous affliction that says the wrong thing.
- Don't stroke your chin: still another nervous gesture that can put off a client.
- Don't scratch. So many people do this without being aware of it. It's likely to make the client itch!
- Don't bite your nails or pull at the cuticles on your fingers. Believe it or not, some people do this while selling!
- Don't jingle coins in your pocket as you talk.
- Final don'ts: Don't doodle or toy with things. Picking things

up and putting them down, unwinding paper clips, twisting pencils and fidgeting with pens, playing with your ring—these are all nervous mannerisms that can annoy your client.

IT'S THE SIZZLE THAT SELLS THE STEAK

I have a good friend, Jim, who's long past the half-century mark. Jim spent most of his life in sales, and then became CEO in charge of sales for a nationwide organization. He's retired now, doing consultant work, but he likes to talk about the "good old days," and most of what he says is very applicable to what concerns us today.

"I started out working with the president of the Tested Selling Institute in New York City. That was back in 1942. He knew all about subtext way back then. His favorite line was 'It's the sizzle that sells the steak, not the cow!' Though, to tell you the truth, I think the cow's pretty important."

I asked Jim to explain that. "Well, you never saw a cow walk through a restaurant enticing the customers to carve themselves a sirloin. But let a waiter carry a sizzling platter of steak through, and everyone's mouth waters. Now everything you sell has to have a sizzle. You find the sizzle in your product and you're halfway home!

"Once you've got that down," he went on, "you need a touch of showmanship. You know, what you do is as important as what you say. The way you move your hands and feet, the way you touch the product, that's all important. Watch that eyebrow. Lift it in surprise, and you can lift yourself right out of a sale. You've got to be sincere. Your smile has to be sincere without becoming a smirk. You have to send out an impression."

"A subtext?"

"Exactly. A subtext that says you're pleased by the customer, pleased with your product, glad to have a chance to sell it, confident about an order."

Once I related the idea of subtext to Jim's "sizzle" I began going over some of the showmanship techniques he once used in order to sell.

When he sold insurance, he stressed the subtext of the money that the policy would provide for leisure and travel. To get that sizzle across, he'd show his client pictures of distant, exotic places—Hawaii, Japan, Kenya. When he sold men's suits he'd tie a string and a weight to a button to show that it wouldn't come off. This kind of showmanship created strong subtexts in the client's mind—the sizzle that sold the steak.

GIVING TWO CHOICES

My six-year-old granddaughter was a bit too bright for her mother, and hoping for some advice, my daughter consulted a psychologist: "I can't get her to do what I tell her to."

"What you have to do with children that age," the psychologist advised, "is give them two choices. They'll always take one."

Dubiously, my daughter tried it out one night when the child wouldn't clean up after playing. "You have two choices. Pick up your toys or go to your room!"

My granddaughter looked thoughtful, then said, "I don't like either of those choices. Is there another one?"

Well, she's a bit cagier than most people. A real estate sales-woman uses the two-choice method very successfully. She told me about a doubtful client to whom she was showing two condos on the thirty-second floor of a New York building. She felt that she was ready to zero in and clinch the sale. Inside one condo, she said, "This has a magnificent view of the Hudson, hasn't it?" The client agreed. When they looked at the other, similar condo, she said, "Here's another magnificent view. The East River." Again the customer agreed. "Which view would you prefer?" my real estate friend asked. The client looked out the window. "Oh, the Hudson River, of course." That did it. She was on her way to a commitment.

In selling, it is a good idea to give the potential buyer a choice between something and something else, never between something and nothing. Then, with a leading question, you can get a commitment of sorts, and you'll be ready to sell.

Another technique in selling is not to fight the would-be buyer. If the buyer disagrees about one point, think about it a moment, then: "I see your point, but . . ." And then get into the sales pitch. You send out a subtext of agreement. You are on the buyer's side, and that tends to temper any hostility.

But in using this technique, be sincere. Understand that there is probably something valid about the objection. Examine it and find a way around it, but don't deny it. That sends a subtext of "I know better than you," and even if you do, you don't want the buyer to think so. Agree, then explain: "I'm glad you brought that up," or "Most shrewd buyers ask me that," or "Yes, you're right. I was going to explain that."

I'M THINKING SERIOUSLY OF BUYING

One final subtext that every good salesperson must learn is the one that signals when the client is ready to buy. Too often sellers let these subtexts escape. You have to be alert in order to grasp and understand them. My retired salesman friend speaks of his mentor once again.

"He used to divide these signals into two parts, the spoken ones and the unspoken ones. Let me give you a few examples of spoken signals. These are the ones you listen for. When you hear them, you stop your pitch and ask for the order.

" 'How is that cosmetic made?'

" 'Will that metal tarnish?'

" 'Will the material stand up under everyday wear?'

" 'Can I take these outside and look at them under the light?'

"People ask questions like these when they're thinking out loud about buying. When you get this type of question, the subtext says, 'I'm ready to buy.' Don't waste time or spoil the sale by continuing with your pitch."

The best of these signals relate to money!

"Can I pay monthly instead of weekly?"

"Would I save anything by buying in bulk?"

"Are they all the same price?"

"What kind of a break can you give me in price?"

"How much deposit do you need?"

Don't ever pass by the price question. The subtext is pretty obvious: "I'm just about ready to buy!"

Other signals are the more subtle ones of body language, my friend explained. "We knew all about that back in the forties, though we didn't call it body language until *you* coined the name. Mainly, we looked at the customer's eyes. I believe the eyes really *are* the mirror of the mind. Mostly, customers try to keep a poker face and not let you know what they're thinking, how interested they are. But when their eyes keep looking at the samples or at the contract on the table, they're interested! Pick it up and talk about it, explain it. When the customer asks 'How does this work?' or 'Where does this come from?' or better yet, 'What I need this for is . . .' then you're home free!

"I'll tell you some more unspoken or body language signals. When customers' eyes are half-shut, they're doing some big thinking about buying. Don't talk too much. They probably aren't listening. But when they purse their lips, they're very close to buying. Then you zero in on the things that interest them and repeat them. Produce your contract. Talk about quantity discounts. That's your big moment. Grab it!"

Here are some other important nonverbal signs:

- The customer keeps handling the contract.
- He scratches his head thoughtfully.
- She toys with a pen.
- He rubs his chin thoughtfully.
- She leans back in her chair, thinking.
- He calls a friend for advice.
- She bites her lip or furrows her brow.

In all these signals, the subtext is the same: "I'm thinking seriously of making a deal."

11

DANGEROUS
LIAISONS

THE MAN WHO LOVED HIS BOSS

"My trouble really began," Art told me, "when I fell in love with my boss.

"I was assistant sales rep, and Simone was head of the department. I was attracted to her the day she interviewed me. There was something about her . . . As if she really cared that I wanted to work there. I know I'm good at my job, but I've never had such a positive response at an interview. And then—there were all kinds of things. Nothing overt, but—well, the vibes were right."

"Vibes?" I asked.

"Well, I know you'd call it subtext, and I guess it was. It was something I couldn't put my finger on."

"You flirted with each other?"

He hesitated. "Flirting is too strong a word. It was a whole group of little things like when we discussed sales strategy. There's nothing romantic in sales strategy, but the way we talked about it, and only to each other, the words we used . . . I'd be stupid not to realize that something was going on."

"What about body language?"

"Well, we'd come in close when we talked about a client, as if we were sharing a secret."

"You mean you shared personal space?"

"Exactly. It was a little strange, at first, but I kind of liked it, and I found myself responding. We were alone in the office one night, going over some contracts. Why were we working late?" He shrugged. "I think it was both our faults. I'd set up a situation where we just couldn't get all the work done in time for the next day's board meeting. She went along with my little conspiracy. And then—it was our first kiss—and our last."

"Why your last?"

"Because I suddenly realized what was going on. Look, she was five years older, a lot smarter, and on her way up. I was just getting started in the firm. Sure, I've heard of people sleeping their way to the top, but I just thought it would be professional suicide. I didn't want a real commitment at that time. Suppose she did? I'd be on the spot if our romance went sour for any reason. I'd be in deep trouble. I did the most sensible thing I could. I backed off and went job hunting right away!"

SLEEPING YOUR WAY TO THE TOP

Is Art's story unusual? If he had started an affair with his boss, could he have used it as a boost up the corporate ladder? Or would it have been a mistake? We've all read the glitzy novels about people who sleep their way up the corporate ladder. But what's the real story?

In a recent poll of one thousand working men conducted by a national magazine, almost half of those thirty-five years or under felt that a man could indeed sleep his way to the top. Those over thirty-five were more doubtful, but still one-third of them felt it could be done; and yet only 6 percent of the men polled say they have tried it.

To pin it down a little more, 71 percent of the men polled had worked for a woman, and a quarter of those said they were sexually attracted to her. A fifth said the boss was attracted to them.

Art, who was forty and divorced, felt that dating his boss would lead to "professional suicide." But more than half of the baby boomers in the poll allowed that they would feel comfortable in such a situation. The generation gap is in strong evidence here.

What about the woman who tries to use sex and its subtext to get ahead? Consider the story of Cynthia and Leslie, stock traders at a brokerage house in Chicago. "We were both hired at the same time," Cynthia recalled, "and there was always some friendly competition between us. It came out in the open when a really good position as vice president in charge of trading opened up. We had the same seniority, and our work was on an equal level, but Leslie dressed in a way that I couldn't help admiring, but would never dare imitate. The signals she sent out were pretty clear.

"We knew the position of vice president would go to one of us, but after the first week I was sure it was Leslie's. She began an all-out campaign to seduce our boss. At first it was just some flirting, but then it was a few lunches together, and finally, she told me smugly, they were going out after work on a real date. I found out later that it ended in a hotel room.

"Well, I figured that was it—the job was hers. But to my surprise she came into my office a week later in tears. What was wrong? The boss had told her she was fired! He just couldn't work with her after what happened. He'd give her a good reference, but only if she kept quiet about their affair.

"I felt bad for Leslie, but I was thrilled when the boss told me that the position was mine. It was the first time I realized my low-key image might be an advantage."

Cynthia's "low-key image," which she had sometimes wished she could change, sent out a subtext about her ability to do the job well. True or not, we often assume quiet, unassuming people are more efficient than sociable, flashy ones. Although Leslie was just as good a worker, her extroverted style had a different subtext. She was "available," and her flirting made that clear. It was easy enough for her boss to respond, but while he may have felt that a one-night stand was okay, he wasn't about to let a relationship complicate his job. Leslie had misread his subtext.

SEXINESS IN THE CORPORATE WORLD

In actuality, it wasn't Leslie's "style" that did her in, although her style sent out a subtext of availability. It was her assumption that she could parlay that subtext into a promotion by sleeping with the boss.

Helen Gurley Brown, editor of *Cosmopolitan* magazine, has had a wealth of experience in the workplace. Although her ideas go against most viewpoints, they are worth mentioning because of her success.

Gurley Brown's very strong feeling is that it's altogether good and proper and advantageous for a woman to send out a subtext of sexiness in the corporate world. In her book *Sex and the Office* she suggests that provocative clothes can be a "secret weapon" for the businesswoman. Among her recommendations is "boy tailoring" on a woman's "curvy" body. She feels that the contradiction is arousing. She also advocates revealing dresses and stimulating perfumes.

But she seems to be alone in her advocacy. Almost every other authority on working women feels that any subtext of availability on the job will inevitably backfire.

If an office romance holds danger for a woman, it is equally dangerous for a man. Unless the relationship is a serious affair that will end in a real commitment, it leaves him vulnerable to obvious problems: Other workers will soon be aware of what's going on and will resent it; his own supervisors will probably frown on the arrangement; and he cannot expect the same kind of working relationship with a lover as he could have with someone less personally involved.

THE END OF THE AFFAIR

Dating the boss, male or female, or dating anyone whose position is above yours, is only part of the problem. The really tough part is putting an end to such an affair. The person higher on the corporate scale usually sees the best solution as getting rid of the other partner. The question of blackmail—"Fire me and I'll spread our affair all around"—is countered by "If you want decent references, play ball!"

Sometimes it's important to get out of an affair before it starts. Ending the affair is a difficult problem, and, as Art sensed, such a quick way to the end of a job that the best possible advice is don't, under any circumstances, date anyone on a higher level than you. Good advice, but since we're all human, it is not always followed.

ROMANCE IN THE OFFICE

Should romance in the office be off-limits altogether? Is there no place for it? The truth is, many marriages and lasting relationships have come out of office romances. The logic runs: What better place is there for a woman to find an eligible man? Or a man an eligible woman? It is only when the relationship is out of kilter that danger sets in.

Art, in falling for an older woman higher on the corporate ladder, stepped onto shaky ground. Leslie, in attempting to seduce a man in a higher position in order to get ahead, was in that same danger zone. Leslie's subtext was very obvious, but false. Art's subtext, less obvious, still had a note of insincerity about it. He had no intention of going on to a serious commitment, something his boss was looking for.

On an equal and honest footing, the subtexts can all mesh easily. "I like you." "I want to know you better." "I might even be falling in love." There is nothing wrong with those signals. There is only danger when they interfere with the job or with relationships on the job.

"I would ask out a woman I work with," one executive told me, "but I would do my best to keep it out of the office."

"In my experience," a woman executive told me, "practically every man in our office either has had an affair or is capable of having one."

"Most of the women in the office," one secretary told me, "will date a fellow worker. Sure, some of them marry the men, but not all!"

In my own office experience, I can count at least seven married people who started office affairs. Four of them eventually divorced and were "happier" with their new mates. The other three managed either to have their partners transferred or reassigned themselves when the affairs broke off.

In the long run, I still believe that the office should be off-limits for romance. Letty Cottin Pogrebin, who has had varied experiences in the workplace, agrees. In her book *How to Make It in a Man's World*, she advises workers to nip on-the-job romance in the bud. "It's likely to imperil the job when the sweet talk turns serious." She cites office romance as a hazard that lies in wait for those who mix business with pleasure. Pogrebin advises self-discipline in office relationships and suggests that people look to parties, friends of friends, blind dates, clubs, adult education, or other activities before turning to the office. But she, too, recognizes the driving force of sex and concludes that yes, "you can have an office romance as long as it doesn't interfere with office business."

Many companies disagree with this and have even set up rules against it. Some law firms will actually write an employment contract that prohibits marriage between employees. The Hewlett-Packard Company has a policy that specifically discourages nonworking "relationships" between supervisors and those under them. They feel that there would be a potential conflict of interest involved.

However, Robert Mathis, the Kayser Professor of Management at the University of Nebraska in Omaha, believes that you can't control Cupid's arrows. "Just as you can't legislate morality, you can't completely outlaw attraction in the office." Still, he thinks that companies should have clear policies about dating.

The Gannett Company faces the reality that sex will be an issue wherever men and women work together. Christine O. Landauer, the company's director of training and development, remarks, "If employees let their personal relationships affect their objectivity in the office, then we deal with the problem. But we would consider it unfair to prejudge the professionals we employ by assuming they couldn't separate their working lives from their *personal* lives."

SEXUAL HARASSMENT

Another way in which sexuality complicates life in the workplace is when harassment becomes a problem. What is office flirting and how far can it go before it becomes harassment? Let's take the case of Jane, a dispatcher for a large construction company in the southeast. Dispatching was a job traditionally held by men, but Jane, a widow with two children, needed the higher salary the job paid and passed the company test ahead of the other candidates. She was a good worker and a cheerful one. "I knew my job, and I did it," she recalls. "I didn't waste time around the office coffee machine."

Jane was an attractive woman, and all the other employees were men. "I don't know when it began to be more than I could take," Jane said. "At first it was jokes, then off-color remarks as I went by. If I complained, I was a poor sport. But I didn't feel that it was just friendly ribbing, and when I refused to go along with it, it became a lot more serious.

"Sometimes, they'd deliberately brush against me as they passed. Sometimes it would be a so-called harmless pat on my behind. I knew the subtext behind all the innuendos and suggestions. It was out-and-out sexual harassment!

"I finally went to the boss to complain. I hated to, but I couldn't handle it. He listened, then looked at me as if I were crazy. 'Hey, it's just the guys. What the hell, they don't mean anything by it. That's just the way the guys are.' "

Jane's experience is not at all unique. In fact, it's a very common situation. The joking and leering seem to be purely sexual on the surface, but there is usually a deeper subtext, especially when a woman is doing a job traditionally viewed as man's work. Then the subtext is envy and anger, a buried male resentment against women striving for equality, a resentment that surfaces as sexual innuendo and is, in reality, sexual harassment.

THE LEGAL ASPECT

Could Jane have taken her case to court? Probably, but it would have been a hard fight. Only a handful of cases brought by women complaining of sexual harassment have produced grounds for legal action. The reason? The courts are often unsympathetic; there is always fear of reprisals; and the resolution of a case can take years, prolonging any emotional turmoil and creating a serious financial drain. Many women are understandably reluctant to become embroiled in such a difficult situation.

But this is changing as women continue to enter the workplace in increasing numbers. Employers, either realizing the importance of women workers and their contribution to business, or aware of a 1986 Supreme Court decision that an employer is legally responsible for preventing sexual harassment and providing a harassment-free environment, are taking the initiative in fighting harassment.

Good Housekeeping points out that in Camden, New Jersey, the Campbell Soup Company began a program shortly after the Supreme Court decision to teach its 1,700 workers just what the court has ruled about sexual harassment and how to handle it. The company spokesperson explained that "it's in the company's own interest to prevent problems and quickly solve the ones that do occur."

Campbell isn't the only company taking action. Among others, Du Pont, in Wilmington, Delaware, uses half-day seminars to teach its 100,000 company employees the subtexts of sexual harassment and what help is available.

Freada Klein, a human-resources consultant from Boston, justifies these training policies. "Companies need to reach out to their employees to say it's okay to speak up," she says, explaining that even when there is a policy against harassment, some women are afraid to come forward.

There are advantages, not only to a company that discourages sexual harassment, but also to its workers. K. C. Wagner, a Manhattan-based consultant who does corporate training on sexual harassment, says that problems resolved within the company result in less damage to workers' careers and emotions.

One important factor is understanding just what sexual harassment is. What are the subtexts that clue you in to when it's happening? The difficulty is that there are very few objective subtexts. Sometimes the harassment is obvious, but far more often it exists in a gray area that boils down to one person's perception versus another's.

Good Housekeeping points out that, legally, there are two kinds of sexual harassment: "Unwelcome verbal or physical conduct of a sexual nature used as an outright or implied basis of one's employment or advancement," and "A hostile or intimidating work environment created by sexual jokes, teasing or comments, or even the presence of suggestive posters."

Behind the teasing, the suggestions, the posters, there is the subtext that says "Women do not belong here, or if they do, they are to be used by men."

THE OTHER SIDE OF THE COIN

It seems, from everything written about sexual harassment, that it is a one-way street—that women are harassed by men, but men are never harassed by women. In general, because of the way our society is set up, this is true. Sexual harassment of men does occur, but very rarely and only in extreme circumstances.

Kenneth is a young accountant working in a real estate office in a large city. He handles the computer setup and the accounting details, and he recently decided against filing a sexual harassment suit only because he felt it would make him an object of derision.

"I'm the only man in an office of twenty women, and believe me, it's no bed of roses! I thought, when I first took the job, that I'd like working with a group of women. But I have to tell you, they come on to me all the time. It may be teasing, and if I complain, they pass it off as that. What's wrong with a little harmless flirtation?

"Well, I'm a married man, and I don't think it's harmless. They'll come up to my desk, lean over my shoulder, sometimes even breathe in my ear. They may think they're kidding, but I get a very raunchy message from them, and I don't like it! It goes on all the time, and it upsets me. I can't work to my fullest capacity. I've complained to the boss, but she just laughs at me. I know, men have been doing it for years and it's time we got a taste of it, but I haven't been doing it, and I don't want to take the blame for all men!"

Eventually, Kenneth solved his problem by quitting and finding another job.

FIGHTING SEXUAL HARASSMENT

Male or female, what can you do to fight sexual harassment? First of all, confront the harasser. If it's a man, let him know he's behaving in an offensive way. If this doesn't work, then the next step should be to tell him you'll notify your superior or his superior. It's best to do this in writing. It is also important to keep a written record of what is going on with dates and times of harassment and an explanation of just what is happening. You should keep copies of your records and memos.

If it continues beyond this, you must take the matter to the company heads, reminding them that the corporation is legally responsible for keeping a harassment-free atmosphere. If there is a company complaint procedure, use it.

If all this fails to work, the next step should be to contact your state department of labor or human resources. You can get the telephone number of your Equal Employment Opportunity Commission field office by dialing 1–800-USA-EEOC. They will advise you, and tell you when to file on a federal level.

These steps are often frightening ones to most workers, and, of course, must be considered carefully before they are taken. But if the subtext of harassment is strong and doesn't let up, the employee should take legal action.

12

WHEN WORLDS
COLLIDE: SUBTEXT
AND THE GLOBAL
WORKPLACE

THE AMERICAN BUSINESSMAN AND
THE SAUDI PRINCE

Because today's global marketplace often makes doing business
an international venture, understanding the subtextual language
of other cultures has become a vital job skill. A story is told of
an American businessman sent to Saudi Arabia to negotiate an

oil deal with one of the four thousand Saudi princes. He was finally able to arrange an interview to fit into the prince's crowded schedule. It took place in a large ballroom just before a reception. Eager to make his point, the American started his pitch.

The prince, interested in the project, moved within six inches of the American's face. But the American was uncomfortable at this close encounter, and moved back until there was what he considered a comfortable four feet between them.

The prince moved into the distance at which he felt comfortable, six inches, and the American moved back again, unaware of what he was doing. In this way, the two men, in the next fifteen minutes, covered the entire floor of the ballroom while they talked, the American moving back, and the prince moving forward.

The prince, however, became increasingly unhappy. The subtext he was receiving was clear to him: "I don't want to be close to you. You offend me. I dislike you." The businessman, too, began to feel uneasy. Why was this man getting so unpleasantly close, breathing in his face? He could actually smell the food the prince had eaten. He even felt a disturbing sexual subtext to this closeness, and he found himself stumbling, reddening, and looking away. In the end, the deal fell through. No matter how profitable the collaboration would have been to both men, the subtext of each annoyed the other.

The different needs and desires for space in Saudi Arabia and in the U.S. reflect two different cultures. Almost every culture has its own rules for handling space, and in each a different subtext is sent out when space is invaded.

In the United States and in England, people prefer a two-foot bubble of space around them. When two people talk, the "bubbles" touch, and there is a four-foot distance. This sends out a comfortable subtext. In any social situation, people arrange themselves so that their zones of privacy are intact.

The poet W. H. Auden, in *Prologue: The Birth of Architecture*, recognized this and knew what subtext was sent out when the zones are invaded.

> Some thirty inches from my nose
> The frontier of my person goes,
> And all the untilled air between,
> Is private *pagus* or demesne.
> Stranger, unless with bedroom eyes
> I beckon you to fraternize,
> Beware of rudely crossing it:
> I have no gun, but I can spit.

Private space should only be intruded on by a lover, according to Auden. Anyone else is suspect. It's no wonder that the American businessman saw the prince's intrusion into his space disturbing and sexual. In truth, however, people in the United States also accept intrusion by close friends and loved ones without perceiving a sexual subtext.

HOW DIFFERENT CULTURES HANDLE SPACE

The way we handle space has a direct effect on how we perceive and send out subtexts. In dealing with other cultures, we should be aware of how each handles space.

Arabs, as the prince in our anecdote indicated, are comfortable with a space of six inches between them when they talk. The Arabs like to touch one another. When possible, Arab homes are large and airy, but the residents cluster together in one small area.

In public, Arabs have little concept of privacy. An Arab will push into line and consider this acceptable behavior. When an Arab wishes to be alone, he will simply withdraw into himself. Americans, interacting with Arabs, consider this withdrawal insulting. In Germany, there is a pressing need for private space. During World War II, when German prisoners of war held in the Midwest were housed four to a small hut, they went to great lengths to find material to build partitions so that each man could have his own private space. In Germany, private space—screened balconies and fenced-in gardens—is held sacred.

In German offices and homes, doors are usually kept closed. In American homes they are usually left open—except in teenagers' rooms. During adolescence there is often an overwhelming need for privacy. Americans will shut themselves up in their own rooms when they want to be alone.

The English internalize their barriers in an attempt to find privacy. The English attitude arises from a culture that does not have a great deal of space. Because of this, being close to someone physically does not mean that two people are friends. Sociologist Dr. Robert Sommer, in his book *Personal Space*, quotes an English host talking to an American visitor. "Forgive us our seemingly cold indifference. This is a small and crowded island. We exist only by ignoring each other."

The French, too, are crowded—more so than the Northern Europeans. But in France the crowding evidences itself in a love for the outdoors, for sidewalk cafés. The home is for the family; the outdoors is for socializing and business. On a business trip to France, very little of my work was done at the host's office, and none at his home. Almost all of it was conducted in restaurants and cafés where long, elaborate discussions about the food took place before we got down to business.

In Japan, where space is also at a premium, people have solved the problem by putting a different psychological interpretation on space. Crowding together is considered a sign of a warm and pleasant intimacy. In certain situations the Japanese actually prefer crowding.

Handling space is only one of the ways in which cultures differ subtextually, and only one of the arenas in which a little subtextual language skill can make a big difference in earning big profits internationally. In preparing this chapter I spoke to many business-people who had worked and traveled all over the world. Rather than trust one person's judgment or observation I insisted on inter-views from at least five different people for each country before I settled on the person whose experiences I believe to be most representative.

Since I was dealing with many variations in subtext, I was reluctant to see any trait as a national characteristic unless it was cited a number of times in different situations. Even then, there are always exceptions to the rule, and what seems to be prevalent in any country may not apply to everyone.

Almost all the businesspeople asked me not to use their names or accreditations since they were still doing business in these countries or acting as consultants to Americans doing business abroad. I have respected their wishes for anonymity, but I have told their stories with great exactitude. Here are their experiences.

EXPERIENCING THE SAUNA

John, a citizen of the United States, is a professor of management at an outstanding university and has had thirty years of business experience. For the last ten years he has been an international consultant. I asked John about his experience doing business in various European countries and the different subtexts he found there.

In describing Scandinavia, he noted that the Danes are very much like the North Americans. "They have a good sense of humor, but they know when to be serious. As for subtext, what you say is what they perceive. There are very few subliminal messages."

By contrast, he pointed out, the Swedes are very aloof. "They are not about to accept you on your own terms, and it takes a great deal of time for you to establish a relationship with them. They don't engage in prolonged conversations. If you ask, 'How's the weather?' a Swede will answer, 'It's fine.' Nothing beyond that.

"With the Danes, when you ask about the weather, they'll settle back and start with, 'What part of Denmark are you interested in?' and it goes on from there."

I was most intrigued when he talked about the Finns. Finland is a bilingual country with Finnish and Swedish as its two languages. Unfortunately, though John could speak Swedish, few Finns were willing to use it in business meetings. They all spoke Finnish, a difficult language related to almost no other in Europe. In business negotiations, John found the Finns very tough, very specific, and very demanding. The subtexts they sent out to him were "We are a closed society. We do not trust any outsider."

"I was there on business," John explained, "at Rosennew, the biggest foundry in Finland, I was trying to get them to make a line of enamel-on-steel cookware. Most of their products were castings for heavy farm equipment, but they did have some consumer products, and I knew they could turn out what I wanted.

"The trouble was, I was getting nowhere. We just couldn't negotiate a price. They wouldn't understand who we were as a company, and they really didn't care to understand. They were more interested in my understanding who they were.

"While we were talking and getting nowhere, in an attempt to make small talk, I asked about the sauna, a national phenomenon in Finland. No other Scandinavian country had it to any degree.

"For the first time in our talks they seemed to come alive, and they explained that since their country was so bitterly cold, the sauna was a good place to keep warm and to discuss business. When I told them I'd never been in one, they tentatively invited me to have our next meeting there. I realized they weren't sure how I'd take the invitation. How do you invite an American to get undressed to come to a business meeting? I began to understand that a lot of their business is actually conducted in the sauna!

"When I accepted the invitation, they were pleased. We went into the sauna, stripped to the buff, and they began to discuss business. There was a lot of joking, and an easy camaraderie developed. All of them spoke Swedish for my benefit. To my delight, I got through just what I wanted to. It was a totally different relationship!"

The subtext, John realized, was obvious: "We don't trust you until we understand that you won't laugh at our ways or look down on us as many foreigners do." But there was another, more subtle, subtext in the sauna meeting: "When you are naked, you have nothing to hide! You are willing to expose yourself. There was a sense of equality among us. Dress, position, even aggressive boardroom moves were forgotten. We were definitely on the same level."

John found that getting into the sauna established trust. "Once I realized what was going on," John explained, "I accepted other elements of their culture. They believe that Americans eat only steak and look down on reindeer eaters. They were pleased when I ordered reindeer meat as my main course during dinner. They became more open, and I was more at ease. The barriers between us dissolved."

BUSINESS IN GERMANY, FRANCE, AND BELGIUM

The Germans, John told me, in many ways do business like the Finns, in the sense that they are tough, specific, and demanding. But that, he emphasized, is now. "I first went to Germany to do business in the early fifties. They were still recuperating from World War II, and we were the conquerors. We could do no wrong, and they were eager to shed their guilt and tell us how sorry they were. The subtext: 'We are out to please you at any price.' "

However, returning to Germany in the sixties, John found that things had changed drastically. "In Hamburg I met the same people I had met twelve years ago. They were prosperous, and the war was in the past, forgotten. They talked down to us in business dealings because they were dealing from a position of power. The subtext was 'We are the top guys!'

"In Germany today, they believe in candor. They no longer worry about hurting your feelings. If you put out a proposition that they think is terrible, they'll tell you right out what they think of it. The subtext is 'We have the power and the strength. You meet us on our terms.' "

France is quite different, according to John. "It's very regional, and doing business there requires different strategies, and you run into different subtexts depending on whether you're up north or down south, east or west. The closer I got to the Belgian border, for example, the more provincial I found the people to be. It was almost impossible to hold a discussion on a factory level. Why? Because there was no contest. You could win in any negotiation. Their subtext was 'We're uneasy because you're tougher and more knowledgeable than we are.'

"However, that was in the provinces. As you get closer to Paris, doing business is like doing business in America. The only hurdle is the language. There's been a lot of talk about the French refusing to have anything to do with you if you don't speak French. I never found that to be true. In fact, if you knew the language, they were tough negotiators, but if you didn't, they would go out of their way to make you feel at ease and help you. If you spoke the language, the subtext was 'You are on our level. Let's slug it out!' If you didn't speak French, the subtext was 'We'll help you get over the difference between us.' "

John had done some business in Belgium, and he saw the Belgians as "poor Frenchmen," who try to emulate the French, but never quite succeed. "Their standard of living," he said, "is lower than that of the French, and they have more trouble with our language. In French industry, you could always find someone who spoke English. Not in Belgium. Outside the cities, you had to rely on interpreters, and there's one big problem with interpreters. There is no subtext!"

John explained what he meant. "An interpreter never editorializes. He or she simply takes your words and translates them as literally as possible, and that leaves out all of the nuances—and all of the subtext."

JAPAN

In Japan, however, the reverse is true. According to Cathy, a woman in her thirties who speaks Japanese fluently and has spent many years as a business consultant in Japan and America, you can ask a Japanese businessperson a question through an interpreter, listen to a half hour of back-and-forth talk between interpreter and businessman, and then have the interpreter tell you, "He doesn't think he can do it."

The long exchange is an attempt to evaluate you, the short reply is the outcome of that analysis. "The Japanese are very concerned with what sort of person you are. How do you think? Can you be trusted? All of that is part of the translation, which, of course, you never hear. You receive a filtered-down version. Actually, you get the subtext. They do a great deal of editorializing."

A point to remember when doing business in Japan, Cathy points out, is that the Japanese never want to hurt your feelings. In a business deal, things may look good to an American if he or she is taken out and wined and dined. The American sees the subtext as "The deal is going through." In fact, this wining and dining can have just the opposite subtext.

"I ran my own consulting business in Japan," Cathy told me, "and at one point a Japanese bank wanted to branch out. An American attorney who had hired me hoped to convince these bankers to retain him. After a long business meeting, the head of the Japanese bank took us out for a very expensive lunch. My client was sure that he was their man. Why else would they insist on such a long and lavish lunch?

"As we left the restaurant, I thanked the banker, in Japanese, and with a slight bow, he said, 'It's the least we can do.' I knew it was his way of saying, 'No deal.' "

One of the most important subtexts in Japan has to do with age. Older people in Japan, unlike in America, are venerated and treated with great respect. Cathy told me of a young "hotshot"

American lawyer who spoke Japanese and was respected by his Japanese colleagues. He worked for a Japanese law firm, but they wouldn't let him service his Japanese clients alone because he was only in his thirties. His firm knew that the clients would be insulted unless a more experienced attorney was present at meetings. The older lawyer, whether he was capable or not, gave a subtext of authority to the meetings.

"There are many subtleties in dealing with the Japanese," Cathy stressed. "Exchanging business cards is one area that can cause problems. In the United States, you take someone's business card. Perhaps you glance at it, then you put it in your pocket.

"In Japan, that would have all the subtext of an insult. You must take the card, study it and make some complimentary comment about it. Then you place it on the table and leave it there for some time. Put it away too soon and you've insulted the owner. The subtext would be 'This person is not important.'

"We Americans see Japan as moving at a slower pace. We are often frustrated because they take a long time to make decisions. Here in the States, a top executive will make a decision and impose it down the line. In Japan, there is a committee, and everyone on it has input into that decision. Each person reads the document with the decision and stamps it with a seal. They don't sign things as we do. They use a stamp cut out of ivory with characters engraved on it. The seal carries the same subtext that a signature does here. 'I agree to this.'

"In fact, you can give someone else your stamp to withdraw money from a bank, and the bank will accept it!

"Because so many opinions are needed to make a decision, and because the Japanese favor compromise and consensus, meetings can seem endless, and there will be meeting after meeting until consensus is reached. You have to be prepared for the long haul if you do business in Japan."

It is also important, according to Cathy, that people of equal rank sit next to one another at business meetings. The head of the table with the seat of honor goes to the most important person. "The seat of honor in a traditional Japanese meeting room," Cathy notes, "is with your back to an alcove with a pleasing flower arrangement, a must in any business setting. Americans would think it more flattering to be seated facing the alcove so you could see the flowers."

There are subtle nuances of speech you must be aware of at Japanese business meetings, according to Cathy. When someone says "We'll think about it," he or she is actually saying "No!" At a table in a restaurant, when you are asked if you would like another drink, you don't say "No, thank you." That would hurt the host's feelings. Instead, if you don't want the drink, you say "I'm fine."

In general, the Japanese culture uses politeness as a universal subtext and as a mask. It is a very hierarchal society, and everyone must know his or her place. Bowing, smiling, and mannered politeness send out not-so-subtle subtexts necessary in a society where crowding is universal. Oddly enough, in this crowded society, touching is frowned on. The American habit of an arm around the shoulder or a touch on the arm is abhorred.

I had always heard that women were excluded from business in Japan, but Cathy assured me that this is not so. "If you're a foreigner, man or woman, you won't fit into the system. But if you're qualified, they'd just as soon deal with a woman as with a man. I know."

As for Japanese women, it is not impossible for one to have a business career. What is impossible is to have such a career and still be married. They feel you should do one thing and do it right. They don't believe you can be a wife and a mother and still work.

"I was the most junior member of a Japanese firm," Cathy said, remembering her early days in Japan. "When we went out to lunch, the most important man would leave first, and after him, each would leave in order of importance. I'd go last and have to push the door open myself. The subtext was clear. I was low woman on the totem pole!

"Then a British attorney visited us, and we all went out to lunch, and lo and behold, they held the door open for me to go out first! I realized that it was because they thought that was what the British visitor would have done, and they didn't want to offend him."

MORE DEALINGS WITH THE JAPANESE

Anthony works for an import furnishings outfit, and frequently travels abroad to arrange for import of various items from different factories. He told me of his problems with a Japanese casting factory. "I went there to see if they could make a certain zinc die cast for a candlestick. We intended to silverplate the casting because that would allow for fine sculpting, depending on how the die tools were made.

"At the factory, I saw that they made excellent die castings for industrial products. I showed the factory committee the sample candlestick and asked, 'Can you do this?' They said yes and I asked how soon can I get samples. They asked when I was leaving Japan. 'In four days,' I told them. 'We'll have the samples for you before you go,' they assured me.

"Now I knew that was impossible. The tools are the key to making a good die cast. Making a good tool is hard work and takes far longer than four days. I told the committee, through my translator, that they couldn't get a tool made in four days. There was a lot of back and forth talk between the committee and my translator, and finally I was told, what they are trying to say is that if they had a tool, they'd get the candlestick in four days.

"Why didn't they say that? Well . . . He couldn't answer that, but I knew the real reason. They didn't want to hurt my feelings. I might feel disturbed if they told me the truth, and I might even go to a competitor. They'd rather lie to me and tell me what I wanted to hear. Had I accepted the four day assessment, I'd return to find it not ready. If I said, 'But you told me four days!' they'd say, 'Very sorry. Unforeseen difficulties.' "

In doing business in Japan, Anthony stressed, you must understand that subtext, "We do not want to hurt your feelings." To break through the subtext, you must phrase your questions properly. Don't ask "How soon can I have the sample?" The time you stay in Japan would determine the answer. The questions should be: "How long will it take you to make a set of tools?" "Do you make the tools here, or do you subcontract them out?" "What will they be made of?" All these details will help you to pinpoint the real answer.

According to all the people I have talked to, there are two languages in Japan. One has a subtext that says "We want you to be happy," and the other has a subtext of reality. To get at that subtext, your questions must be specific, not general.

The Japanese habit of wanting to make the customer feel good can be a defeating one. You can't run a modern business by continually disappointing your customers. To compensate for this, the Japanese have established the Trading Company concept. The Trading Company is essentially an administrative group of people with some technical background in the industry they represent. A Trading Company will represent some ten to twelve factories. It handles the administration work and the invoicing. When you finish playing games at the factory level (a necessary step) you go to the Trading Company for realistic information on prices and delivery. The Trading Company will only do business on an open account. They deal with letters of credit to ensure that they get paid if they live up to their contract.

In a Trading Company, the mask of politeness is partially dropped. They aren't too concerned about hurting your feelings, but to make up for harsh reality, they entertain lavishly. They would think nothing of spending a thousand dollars for a dinner—of course, the factory pays!

KOREA AND TAIWAN

Another businessman, who dealt with Korea, said that negotiating with Koreans was very difficult because they are constantly trying to second-guess you. "For some reason, they feel inferior in negotiations compared to people from the United States. They consider an American an ace negotiator because of his or her education, background and wealth. They are slow to take your word, and they spend a great deal of time boxing with you until they feel they can understand your motives and whether you're sincere."

In Korea this businessman visited a foundry where he wanted to get some decorative brass wall hooks made. The foundry was very archaic, like foundries in the United States 150 years ago, but it turned out beautiful products. Labor, of course, was very cheap.

He showed them his blueprints with the understanding that since they made similar products they could gauge a realistic price. They quoted thirty cents, which he knew was grossly under value.

"Astonished, I repeated 'thirty cents?' That gave me away. They quickly said, 'Well, that's for the one we're showing you. Yours would be higher.' 'How much higher?' 'It depends . . .' We went back and forth, like a boxing match, while they tried to psyche me out. I got the subtext, 'It's going to be cheap, but we want to know how high we can goose you.' In the meantime, I tried not to give them my subtext—'I'll pay much more than you quoted.' "

In Korea, my friend found two types of businesses: the very small company, like the one he ordered the wall hooks from, and the very large company employing up to forty thousand people. The bigger the company, the more it resembled an American corporation, and the easier it was for him to read the subtext. "Talk to a Korean official running a steel factory employing ten or twelve thousand people and it's like talking to a guy from Pittsburgh. The text and subtext are pretty much the same."

This same man did a lot of business with Taiwan. There, he said, you can negotiate anything, but you must also be ready to second-guess everything. "It's a country where certainty doesn't really exist in business. Even when it's signed, you're never sure you have a contract.

"Now big businesses like RCA and GM have their own people working there. They would rather not have the Chinese run the plant. The Chinese in Taiwan are skillful, very good learners, and can be taught to do almost anything, but I hate to do business there no matter what the saving in labor cost. Their subtexts are always confusing.

"For example, if you want an item for thirty cents and they

offer forty, and, after negotiation, you get it to thirty-five—which you can afford—you still won't have a firm commitment. If you ask them how long they can hold that price, they'll tell you they aren't sure. You get a lot of ifs and buts. If I tell them I can't have an open contract, they'll ask me how many pieces I want. I'll tell them fifty thousand, and they'll come back with 'We can probably hold it for fifty thousand.'

"Probably?

" 'Well, we can't be sure.'

"No matter how you try to pin them down, they always slip away, and even with a firm commitment, the next shipment can come through with an invoice a few cents above the agreed price. They only tell you the probabilities, which you can be sure will change. Oh, you can do business there, as long as you understand the subtext behind the contract: 'Somehow or other we're going to up the price!' "

THE ITALIAN WAY

Samantha, a woman in her fifties who travels through Europe buying products for a chain of stores in the States, has had a lot of experience in Italy. "They do make beautiful things, but the Italians south of Milan, I must tell you, are almost naive in their business dealings. They fully intend to stick to what they promise, and their subtext seems to be transparent honesty and a deep desire to accommodate you. You have to know that.

"You find an item you want, and they'll promise you delivery in three months. Just what your schedule needs. The trouble is, you won't get the delivery then. They promise you anything to get the order because they know, if they get it, they'll get some payment. You may not continue to do business with them, but they'll get something."

Samantha told me she had dealt with a very famous Italian dinnerware manufacturer, who has a wholly owned subsidiary in the States. "I think the parent company has sales of a billion dollars, and the subsidiary sells twenty million. That's pretty small in terms of the parent company, and so they treat it as nothing and lie to their own subsidiary. They'll send cups without saucers. The subsidiary can't use a cup without a saucer. Okay, they say, they'll send it next week. When the order comes through, the saucers are still missing. Now that's their own subsidiary. Imagine what it's like if you aren't a subsidiary!

"The only difference is when you deal with a cooperative. Then the plant manager has a sense of responsibility and you'll get a realistic price and delivery on time."

Are there any tricks to doing business in Italy? I asked her, and she shrugged. "I never found out how to be successful there. Now I simply assume that if they tell me delivery will be in three months, I figure six. I compensate. You know, I've even tried doing business there with a letter of credit with an expiration date. No difference. They'll let it expire. They feel that if you buy on a letter of credit, then you're locked in. Your subtext tells them you'll give in before they do. They let the letter of credit be canceled, and they wait for you to say, okay, let's extend it. That will buy time, but of course it's a risk."

"Is that true all through Italy?" I asked her.

"No. Not in Milan. That's the center of industrial activity. All the businesspeople are located there. The bankers and industrialists there have discovered that they can't survive without some stability. There's more certainty in Milan.

"But the farther one gets from Milan, the more the Milanese

see the people they deal with as peasants. There's a big class distinction throughout Italy. In Sicily, for example, the people call the Neopolitans Northerners. They're talking about people only forty miles away! They think of all Northerners as big industrialists. The truth is, however, that Naples is a poor, devastated city rife with unemployment.

"Now I must point out that there are exceptions. There's Olivetti. Olivetti distributes merchandise all over Italy and they have their own way of doing things. There's an Italian phrase about Olivetti that sums up the policy of the firm. It's *Taco Olivetti*. Roughly, it means the Olivetti way. Somehow they are successful in a very bureaucratic system. The whole industrial setup in Italy is bureaucratic, and it goes right through to the government.

"Don't get me wrong," Samantha added quickly. "They are not dishonest in the way that we know dishonesty. They believe that's the way to do business, and it goes right down through the culture to the stores themselves. Everything is negotiable. There is no set price, except in the supermarkets which are modeled on Western styles."

THE HONG KONG CONNECTION

Elaine is a young woman who has spent six years in Hong Kong working in banking. The business pace in Hong Kong, she told me, is pretty much what it is in New York City, a fast-paced environment. "The people hustle a great deal, and doing business depends largely on personal relationships. A lot of business is done in a social setting rather than in the office, over drinks, over dinner, at the golf course, on a yacht. There are many hostess bars in Hong Kong, and business is conducted there too.

"If you are a foreigner, you must get into that routine. You must remember that going out to dinner, drinking, and eating is a big social thing, more important than it is here."

There is very little cultural life in Hong Kong, Elaine told me, and dining and social engagements seem to take the place of theater and music. Foreigners, however, are rarely expected to reciprocate in terms of entertainment. "They understand that usually you are only passing through."

There is, however, a darker subtext to being a foreigner in Hong Kong. Foreigners are still referred to as "foreign devils" by the native Chinese. Although there is a surface camaraderie, "backslapping, handshaking, a lot of physical contact, in general they do not accept strangers," Elaine remarks. "To get to where the power base is, you have to be an insider. Making friends, even on a superficial level, takes a long time."

I asked how a foreigner could overcome the ethnocentricity of the Chinese in Hong Kong, and Elaine shook her head. "With difficulty. Of course, it helps if you speak the language, which in the business world is usually Cantonese. It also helps if you are a senior partner in your firm, an influential person or an older citizen. Influence and importance helps, but age has a very strong subtext in Hong Kong. Once, on a job interview with a Chinese entrepreneur, an older man, I found that his wife and children, present at the interview, treated him with extraordinary respect. The women were silent, waiting on him and even anticipating his wishes, and his son referred to him as 'The Chairman,' always in the third person."

It is best, Elaine stressed, to act deferential in your dealings with older or important businesspeople. "They won't see it as a sign of weakness or a lack of power. In fact, you would project an offensive subtext if you didn't, and you'd get nowhere in business deals."

Age, rank, and being a man are the three things that send out the most relevant subtexts. "I've been in situations where I was excluded from business discussions simply because I was a woman!" Elaine recalled.

THE RUSSIAN FAILING

Mike is an entrepreneur who has tried to do business in the Soviet Union. "Tried is the operative word," Mike says. "In the States, if the deal has something in it for both of us, it will go forward. In the U.S.S.R., it doesn't make any difference. There is simply no incentive to close a deal. The subtext you get is 'Why should I bother? What good will it do me?' Now I'm speaking of government agencies. Since there is no profit motive, no bonus or payoff, there is no incentive.

"Even McDonald's," Mike recalled, "had a hell of a time setting up their golden arches in Moscow. It took years before they could get some flow or momentum, and even then the Soviets who worked there had to be given lessons in subtext. They had to be taught to smile and wait on customers without insulting them or taking their own sweet time!"

According to Mike, and others who have done business in the Soviet Union, there is a tremendous reluctance on the Soviets' part to put themselves out, and the reason, of course, is that they feel there is no profit or advantage in doing so. "There is also a reluctance to experiment, an absence of innovation and an overwhelming bureaucracy that goes right down from government to individuals. It's very discouraging to a businessperson from the States. Americans read Soviets' subtext as 'I've got my job no matter what I do or don't do.' We throw up our hands, and yet . . ." He hesitated. "It's a market with such potential!"

INDIA

Mike has also done some business in India. "What a difference," he told me. "In India they let you do whatever you want to do. You tell a manufacturer, I want that item for twenty-five cents, and no matter what, you'll get it."

The pervasive poverty in India, according to Mike, forces them to keep their small factories open at any expense. "It's their sole support, and if they lose money on one deal, they'll look for another to make it up.

"Usually, when you start negotiating at a factory, you find that the person you are negotiating with will have some contact with the factory, but he or she is not part of it. That person could be the factory's outside accountant, lawyer, or a business acquaintance, someone who's considered your equal. . . ."

This outsider will do the talking, Mike explained, but you have to read the subtext behind the talk. What they are talking about is not necessarily what will happen on the factory level. "This is tremendously important in making any contract or commitment."

GREAT BRITAIN: CLASS STILL COUNTS

In trying to get at the subtexts of businesspeople in Great Britain, I talked to Ian, who has lived in the States for thirty years and represents an American company abroad.

"I constantly do business with the Brits," he told me, "and there have been great changes there in the past twenty years.

Today, the British businessperson moves far more swiftly than he or she used to, and is quick to understand what you are trying to say. At one time, you had to be a social equal, but that's changing, although it still exists among the older crowd."

Ian pointed out that Great Britain is a country where the subtexts of your speech, clothes, and manners are all of great importance. "The British Broadcasting Company, the BBC, set the standard for proper English speech, and so much revolves around how you speak. Your speech will slot you into the proper social level at once."

I asked Ian what the British thought of the different subtexts of American speech, and he shook his head ruefully. "The Brits have a terrible time differentiating among the American regional accents. All people from the States sound alike to them. However, they do read the subtexts of our clothes and schools. Did you go to Yale, Harvard, Amherst? You're right up there. Do you wear the right cut of suit, the right shirt and shoes? All of that is very important to them in judging character. You see, they tend to wear their characters on their sleeves: a proper school tie, a Savile Row suit, to them the subtext is 'You are a success, you are in an executive position.' "

Another point Ian made is the British liking for ceremony and its subtext. "They like to eat at fancy restaurants. They don't go in for the quick sandwich at their desk as the American businessperson will. In Britain, you wouldn't take a business associate around the corner for a hamburger. Although the very long lunch is out, the executive lunch still lasts from noon to two. There is no power breakfast in Great Britain. They like to linger over breakfast in their own home. If you do have breakfast with a Brit, it will be a social occasion, not a business one.

"British businesspeople like to play their own game, dignified entertainment and the subtext it sends out. They'll make sure there's a bottle of champagne in the visitor's room—the nice little amenities."

If a British businessperson has a nice home, he or she may invite a visitor there for a drink before going out to dinner, or maybe for dinner at home. "They like to show you their homes, unlike the French or the Japanese."

Asking people to visit you for a weekend is still done after an association has been established, according to Ian, but this usually occurs only in the upper levels of society. The visiting person must be of the same social class as the host. The invitation will usually revolve around something they want to show you, like a medieval church, or something they want you to watch, such as a fox hunt or a race. Ian advises that it is good policy to accept such an invitation. "The visit may interest you, but even if it doesn't, it's part of the process of getting to know each other on a nonbusiness level."

For all the social propriety, Ian feels that British businesspeople may be quite ruthless. However, their approach is often determined by the other person's attitude. "They regard Americans as pushy for trying to get at a bottom line or a quick sense of direction in a relationship. They're sensitive about that. They wonder why he or she is in such a hurry. They won't come right out and say so, but they read the subtext 'I am trying to put something over on you,' into Americans' aggressiveness."

The British like to size up the Americans. "They will be interested in your schooling, where you went to university. In your lifestyle—though you should never pull out pictures of your wife and kids. They'll assure you that they're very nice, but what they're really thinking is, 'I wish you wouldn't start all this now!' They are very reserved about their personal lives. In Great Britain you never ask anybody what he or she earns. The Brits have a rather unkind joke about Americans. They say, you meet one and the American immediately asks, How old are you? What do you do? How much do you make?"

To break the ice, Ian suggests asking the British business associate about something that interests you. "If you are a theater buff, you might ask about the latest production of the Royal Shakespeare Company. They'd be quick to tell you about the season's openings and might even invite you to see a performance. The trick is to express your interest indirectly and let them help you."

The British no longer dress for dinner, but if you're invited to dinner or to a country house weekend, it's proper to ask what the dress will be. "They would much rather you ask than to have you arrive dressed incorrectly."

A final warning Ian gave concerns the proper way to address the British businessperson who happens to be a member of the aristocracy. "If he is a knight named John Smith, you address him as Sir John, not Mr. Smith and never Sir Smith. If he is a baron, marquess, earl, or viscount, it will be Lord Smith, not Lord John!"

In Great Britain, as in Russia and the Eastern Bloc countries, change is going on, and many of the subtexts that work this year may be out of date next year. This may be particularly true of Russia, where the attempt to move into a free-market economy could change the workers' attitudes.

AFTERWORD

As this book has shown, the ability to recognize subtext will not only allow you to express yourself more effectively in the workplace, it will also help you to better understand others. In some cases, understanding subtext can be job-saving—provided that you act on what you know.

One man who failed to read subtext in time and act on it was Orville Dale, formerly a labor-relations director at the United Artists

Corporation. According to an article in *The New York Times*, Mr. Dale discovered that his company was going to be acquired by MGM, and he worried about his future in spite of the company's reassurance that there would be no mass dismissal. "They kept telling us not to worry, that everything would stay the same after the merger, that everybody would stay in New York at their same jobs," Mr. Dale remembered.

However, a perceptible, ongoing subtext contradicted the company's overt reassurance and could have clued him in to reality. "We were suddenly using European and other foreign banks for financing, and our budgets for film production costs were starting to dwindle," Mr. Dale said. He also recalled that money in general was getting tight and that employees didn't know who their leaders were, "the UA guys in New York or the MGM people in L.A." Within a year, Mr. Dale, along with other directors, was out of a job. Had he read the situation correctly, Mr. Dale noted, he would have started job hunting at once.

Mr. Dale's case is not unusual. According to a Manhattan executive recruiter, most people like to take the "ostrich approach" and ignore the signals. However, there is no question that if you are willing to attend to them, there are usually perceptible subtextual signals that can help you manage your career. Among the obvious, but too often ignored, signals, this recruiter says, "are things like, you suddenly don't get the same signals that others get; you don't get invited to certain important meetings or social events in the company, or you have to suddenly share your private secretary." These signals, combined with the subtext behind your boss's manner, can give you a clue that it's time to "jump." The important thing is to read them and understand the subtext behind them.

There are times when the subtext lies not in incidents but in words. In case anyone doubts the important subtext behind words alone, consider the unpleasant example of a letter written by a conservative group during the 1990 campaigns and sent to Republican state legislative candidates around the country. The letter included a list of words useful in political campaigns to describe opponents, words such as *liberal, traitors, bizarre, sick, incompetent, corrupt, shallow, pathetic, shame,* and, of course, *tax spending.* Gopac (G.O.P. Political Action Committee), the group responsible for the list, had a good understanding of the intense subtext behind each of these words. "The words and phrases used are powerful," Gopac explained to its candidates. "Read them, memorize as many as possible. And remember that . . . these words will not help if they are not used."

The vast field of subtext goes beyond words and actions to the very appearance of things. This book has discussed how our clothes and our faces send out a subtext to others, but very strong subtexts are also sent out by possessions: a Lexus car, a Gucci bag, a Montblanc pen, a Patek Philippe watch, or a corner office.

The growing recognition of this truth has been responsible for a new business that could well be named Rent-A-Subtext. A Chicago company, understanding the powerful subtext sent out by a businessperson's attaché case, is prepared to rent out a thousand-dollar attaché case for one hundred dollars a day. Its customers, it hopes, will be those businesses who want their representatives to make a particularly powerful impression.

This kind of false façade subverts the best of all purposes behind learning to read subtext: understanding others and projecting a subtext in synch with the best aspects of your own character. In any interaction between people, there is the spoken text and the unspoken subtext. Of the two, the subtext is the more honest because it is usually unconscious. We can lie with words, but it is far more difficult to lie with all the subtextual nuances that accompany those words.

Yet, once we learn the elements of subtext—the signals that accompany our words; speech; the meaning of touch; the language of our bodies and the ethnic, regional, and personal differences in that language; the clothes we wear and the objects we use— we are faced with the temptation consciously to control the subtext we project in order to manipulate others in business and social relations.

Sometimes such manipulation is necessary and good. Sometimes it is immoral and dishonest. And there is always the danger that, even with the best of intentions, conscious manipulation of subtext can become obvious, and thus contradict its intended message.

We should remember that what we communicate with our subtext is most effective when it is unconscious. When our actions, our voices, our appearances all transmit a subtext without our being aware of it, that subtext will be honest, will be perceived as honest, and will be very persuasive.

Just as the salesman in our chapter on selling is at his best when he believes in the product, so we are at our most convincing when we ourselves believe in what we are saying, whether that belief is based on intellectual reasons, on an emotional "gut" feeling, or on a sort of self-hypnosis. Once we believe in our own words, then all manipulative devices become secondary. The unconscious can take over, and our subtext will be as strong and as convincing as our text.

However, this does not mean that a person cannot learn all the elements of subtext and put them to good use. Indeed, we should do just that, for once the elements are learned and incorporated into our behavior, they will surface when they are needed and we can use them convincingly.

INDEX